THE MAN IN THE EMPTY BOAT

THE MAN IN THE EMPTY BOAT

EMPTY BOAT

MARK SALZMAN

OPEN ROAD

INTEGRATED MEDIA

NEW YORK

One

EVERYONE HAS A WORST YEAR; 2009 was mine. I'd been suffering from writer's block for nearly a decade, ever since having children. Fatherhood had filled my heart with joy but turned my mind to mush. When I volunteered for the stay-at-home parent role in our family, I told myself: *I'll write during the kids' naps! Fatherhood will inspire me.* Fatherhood did inspire me, but not to write. When our daughters napped, so did I.

I owed my publisher a book and failed to meet the deadline. When I tried to write, what came out was crap and that made me nervous. In March of 2009, I started having panic attacks. In May of that year, my little sister Rachel became ill with pneumonia. I flew back east to help look after her young daughters while she recovered, but something went terribly wrong during her hospital stay and she never made it home.

When I returned to Los Angeles I was in bad shape. I sought refuge in the comforts of hearth and home, but our family had grown while I was away. We had acquired a dog—and I've never cared for dogs. That dog pushed me over the edge.

Anxiety has been my trademark dysfunction for as long as I can remember. It runs in the family, and it doesn't help that the members of my family are all atheists. Not for us the solace of believing that Someone cares or that suffering serves a higher purpose or that the next world will be better than this one. We are faith-challenged, so perhaps it isn't surprising that we're vulnerable to despair. I've spent most of my life searching for peace of mind, but people with my credentials generally make poor spiritual seekers. Atheists, after all, are supposed to have evolved beyond the need for comforting but unverifiable beliefs. But without comforting beliefs we have no antidote for anguish, and that can be a real handicap.

My search for peace of mind has taken me around the world, prompted me to study Chinese language, martial arts, and philosophy, and ultimately led me to become a writer. In 2009 I found a reason to call off the search. My year of crisis ended with a life-changing epiphany, which sounds good until I describe the incident that triggered it.

My view of the world, of myself, and of life itself was changed forever by the sound of a dog farting.

Two

EIGHT YEARS AGO, A MUSICIAN friend who was in town for a concert invited me, my wife Jessica, and our daughter Ava to have dinner with him at a fancy restaurant. (Esme, our second daughter, was still a year away.) We set Ava up in a high chair with a pad of paper and some crayons, and she got right to work while the three of us grown-ups started talking. An hour later, our friend—noticing that Ava hadn't whined or squirmed or interrupted us at all during that hour—asked what we'd done to make her so serene.

I am a person who has tried just about every method known to man to achieve serenity and none of them has worked, so I said, "She sure as hell didn't learn it from me." This led our friend to pose the following question: Since we inherit so much from our parents, including their genes, and since they play such a crucial role in our early development, do we ever truly grow beyond their influence?

This was no idle question. His father had been a renowned violinist, musicologist, and music teacher whose approach to parenting was authoritarian in the extreme. Once the father recognized that his son had a musical gift, he drove the boy relentlessly. Overseeing every detail of the child's musical career became the man's life's work, his masterpiece, and he was not going to let anyone screw it up—especially not the child himself, who occasionally expressed an interest in doing something other than practicing. Not surprisingly, their relationship became so strained that it eventually broke; for a period of several years, they had no contact at all with each other.

Our friend wrestled for years with questions like: Was what he gained by keeping to his father's schedule for his life worth what he lost? How would his life have been different if he had been allowed/encouraged to make more decisions on his own? When he became a father himself, our friend was determined not to become a controlling parent. But he also knew that sometimes, trying *too hard* to avoid making the mistakes your parents made can have unintended consequences. Renounce cruelty forever and you might become indulgent; forswear emotional distance and you might become overinvolved. How do you break one cycle without setting a new one in motion?

We tossed these questions back and forth for a while until our friend, noticing that Ava was looking at him, asked her, "Well, what do you think?"

I don't think that he really expected an answer from the two-year-old in the high chair—I certainly didn't—but to our astonishment, Ava put her crayon down and said, quietly but firmly, "You are who you choose to be."

Our friend looked thunderstruck, but the way he looked was nothing compared to the way I felt. Only Jessica seemed to take it in stride, but that's mothers for you. They all know their kids are brilliant.

The words weren't Ava's own. She was repeating a line from her favorite movie, *The Iron Giant*. The main character is a robot who was built to be a weapon but doesn't want to be a weapon anymore. He wants to be good like Superman, but only a little boy named Hogarth seems to recognize this; everyone else thinks the robot should be destroyed. In a pivotal scene of the film, Hogarth assures the tormented machine that change is possible. "You are who you choose to be," he says. "You choose."

The robot ends up sacrificing himself to save the humans who want to destroy him. The first time Ava saw the film, she wept as the robot hurled himself at the fatal missile and then asked, between sobs, if she, too, could be like Superman.

"Of course you can," I said, my heart melting.

All right—back to the restaurant. Naturally, I felt the rush of joy that all parents feel when their kids say something that makes them seem clever. I also had the pleasure of knowing that I, who enjoy telling stories more than I enjoy doing just about anything else, would be dining off this one for the rest of my life. At the same time, I felt a twinge of dread. For the first eleven years of being married, I had resisted all suggestions that my wife and I ought to have children. I didn't want us to have kids, because I was afraid that if we did, they might turn out anxious like me rather than calm like their mother. And I can't think of any single idea more likely to generate anxiety and existential paralysis than this one: *You are who you choose to be.* Because if you are who you choose to be, you had better choose wisely, and that's easier said than done.

Three

IF THE SALZMAN FAMILY HAD a coat of arms, it would be a shield
with a face on it and the face would look worried. Jessica once
said to me, "Mark, you were raised by rabbits," and she was right.
Our whiskers tremble when we ponder our uncertain futures. Our
claws are useless for fighting. We live in fear.

My father was a social worker and my mother taught music
out of our home. We lived in a tract house in a peaceful suburb.
We owned a series of reliable Volkswagen buses (the minivans of
their day) and used them every summer to go camping all over the
country. We had few reasons to complain, really, but our whiskers
trembled anyway. We seemed determined to validate Henry David
Thoreau's claim that "the mass of men lead lives of quiet desperation." What were we so afraid of?

Biology may have something to do with it. Anxiety and depression run so strongly through our family that if you were to draw
our family tree, it would look like a weeping willow. When I was
nineteen years old, I became so distraught over what I considered to be the meaninglessness of existence that I dropped out
of college halfway through my junior year. During a visit home
that winter, I found myself confiding all my troubles to my father
while he worked on one of his paintings. He liked to work while

sitting on the floor, with his materials spread all around him, and I found it easier to talk when he wasn't looking straight at me.

My dad has always been a good listener. He doesn't interrupt and he doesn't give advice unless you ask him for it. After he'd listened for an hour or so without interrupting or offering any advice, I began to wonder if he was listening at all, so I asked him if he had anything to say about all this. He was a social worker, after all. He looked up from his painting, pushed his reading glasses a bit higher on his nose, and looked at me for a long time. At last, he gave me a sad little smile and said, "Welcome."

He knew how I felt, because he'd felt that way for most of his life. As a child, he looked so forlorn on most days that his family gave him the nickname Little Old Joe before he'd even reached puberty. His dream as a young man was to become a professional artist, but that dream did not come true. Just after he and my mother were married, the two of them drove from Chicago to New Orleans. My dad tried to find a gallery willing to represent him there, but the experiment failed. They got back in the car and headed east. When the car broke down in Connecticut, my father found work at a family counseling center in Greenwich, my mother took on a few piano students to supplement their income, and I was born two years later, in 1959. My brother Erich came next, in 1962, and our sister, Rachel, brought up the rear in 1963.

When I was ten, my mother realized that due to a fortuitous accounting error, she and my father had saved eight hundred dollars over a period of several years without even realizing it—a huge sum for them. My mother wanted my father to use it to buy himself a telescope. My father had enjoyed stargazing since he was a kid and had always wanted a fine telescope but could never afford one. Now that he had the money, however, my father couldn't bring himself to spend it on a luxury item. He insisted that they use the money to pay down their car loan.

But my mother held firm, and eventually they reached a compromise: Half the money went to pay down the car loan, and with the other half my father bought a telescope. He had to order it in advance, and it took six months before the telescope was completed. I drove with him to Hartford to pick it up at the factory (to save money on shipping), and on the drive home, with this magnificent instrument in the car, I expected my dad to look excited. I'd never seen him buy anything for himself before, and this was something he'd wanted for decades. Instead, he looked grim. I asked him why he looked so unhappy, and he said, "Well, Mark, I'm afraid I've bitten off more than I can chew."

Compared to my father, Mom was our Little Miss Sunshine. Her favorite book as a child was *Pollyanna,* a tale about a little orphan girl who was determined to find the silver lining to every cloud, and my mother certainly tried to live up to that example. But unlike Pollyanna, who liked herself as much as she liked everyone else, my mother's love and light shone outwards only. She was a compulsive perfectionist who could tolerate other people's shortcomings but not her own. A graduate of the Eastman School of Music, where she majored in two instruments simultaneously (piano and oboe), my mother practiced six hours a day, every day, yet invariably felt underprepared for the performances she gave. We always knew better than to talk to her after any of her recitals. She would sit out in the backyard and chain-smoke, staring off into space as she relived every missed note and rushed tempo in her mind. After a few days, she would start practicing again.

When she wasn't practicing, she was cleaning or cooking or organizing the shelves or serving on the local orchestra board. And every afternoon she taught piano for three hours while my siblings and I watched television in the basement. My mother didn't have hobbies; she was too busy for recreation. She lived up to her biblical namesake, the Martha who labored while Mary sat and listened—and like the ancient Martha, my mother ended up believing that Mary had made the better choice. At age sixty-seven, in the final stages of lung cancer (she'd self-medicated with tobacco for fifty years), her fingers became too swollen to practice anymore. She began reading for pleasure, something she'd rarely allowed herself to do when she was healthy. "I should have practiced less and read more," she said to me one day, with an oxygen tube dangling from her nose and a copy of Barbara Tuchman's *The March of Folly* on her lap. "I had it all backwards. But now it's too late."

My sister, Rachel, the youngest of my siblings, was an adorable little girl but so shy that she made herself practically invisible, even at home. She spent most of her adolescence alone in her room, drawing and painting while listening to scratched-up records on a portable LP player.

I drove her to her first dance when she was in high school. When I went to pick her up two hours later, she was in tears. Her date had dumped her the moment she'd arrived, and she'd spent the whole evening by herself in the girls' bathroom. Years later, when she had finished college and had moved back into our parents' house, I tried to play matchmaker and brought home a friend I thought she might like. When my friend and I got there, Rachel was nowhere to be seen; she was experiencing such acute anxiety that she couldn't bring herself to come downstairs to meet him. At the end of the evening, she did appear at the top of the stairs to say good night to us as we left, but there was no follow-up to that mission.

In her mid-twenties, she sought help from a doctor, and happily, the meds he prescribed for her worked. They didn't turn her into Maria von Trapp, but they relieved her symptoms dramatically, and when Rachel wasn't suffering, she savored life. Our brother, Erich, who had earned his CPA but whose ambition was to own and run his own business, proposed that he and Rachel open a custom tile store. The idea was that Rachel would hand-paint the tiles to order and design the installations, while Erich would deal with the customers, the paperwork, and the installation work itself. Their store beat the odds by surviving—but the real surprise came when Erich discovered that our shy sister was shy no longer. It turned out that she had as much talent for customer service as for design and painting. With her anxiety under control, her self-confidence rose, and nothing made her happier than being able to make other people feel good. She'd found a second calling in sales.

Erich, the middle child, was the one who didn't seem to fit the mold. He was born with a shock of red hair, a strawberry-sized birthmark on his forehead, and a disgruntled expression on his face. And boy, could he scream. Our parents named him after Erik the Red, the quick-tempered Viking who cut a wide swath across northern Europe before colonizing Greenland. Our little Viking was a colicky baby who didn't behave like a rabbit at all; if anything, he seemed more like a wolverine cub. As he got older, he simply could not understand what everybody in our house was so worried about. Why didn't our father just quit his job and get one that he liked? And why did our mother practice so much when she could play any piece of music well the first time she read through it?

"It sounds the same as it did six months ago," he would groan as she rehearsed a piece for the thousandth time, and he was not entirely wrong.

He enjoyed sports and competitive board games but couldn't get any of the rest of us to play with him. Trips to art museums and classical music concerts were torments for him, and he was not one to suffer in silence. "Music is boring!" "Art is boring!" He craved stimulation and had a higher tolerance for risk than the rest of us put together. When we drove in the car, he insisted on keeping all of the windows open so that the air could blow on him with maximum force. When he got old enough to drink coffee, he drank it in binges; when he got old enough to drink beer, he did the same.

"Moderation is for monks!" he would bellow whenever our hand-wringing parents advised him to show restraint.

If any of our mother's piano lessons went past six o'clock, or if the student's parents stayed to chat, young Erich would march downstairs into the kitchen and begin rattling pots and pans to signal that class was over. Time for Mom to get those TV dinners in the oven! He despaired over our mother's smoking, and when she admitted that she didn't have the strength to quit, Erich didn't accept her excuse. He decided to take action. He went to a novelty shop and purchased (I doubt you can buy these anymore) a package of tiny, white explosives that he planted inside the cigarettes when she wasn't looking. When she lit the booby-trapped cigarettes, they would emit a loud *pop* and burst open in a shower of sparks. No matter how loudly our father yelled at Erich to throw those goddamned things away, Erich persisted. He didn't like being punished, but he was not afraid of it.

He had, by his own description, an unexciting but untroubled childhood. His grades were good but not great, and he didn't worry about it. He didn't develop any passionate interests in high school or have any tumultuous relationships. He had a crew of loyal friends, and they had a great time together. In his high school yearbook, he wrote "California bound," but beyond that, he didn't have any plans for the future.

Then he got to college, and something in him began to change. He found himself wondering what he was going to do with his life. Since he couldn't identify a specific career that excited him, financial security became the default goal. He majored in accounting and landed a job at a global accounting firm right out of college.

He came home from his first day of work looking shell-shocked. I happened to be visiting that week, so I saw it with my own eyes— he was ashen-faced. The moment he'd walked into that building, he said, he felt as if he had just stepped into someone else's life— and it was the *wrong* life. *How,* he wondered, *did I end up here? What was I thinking?* In short, Erich had finally become a Salzman.

Four

A FINE DESCRIPTION OF WHAT my brother felt that day appears in the glossary of a European existentialist website. It shows up there as a definition for the word *anguish*. I'm not an existentialist; I found the website by accident. I had typed in the search words "French" and "mysterious," but instead of getting photos of Isabelle Adjani, I ended up in a philosophy chat room.

> Anguish: a negative feeling arising from the experience of human freedom and responsibility; the inherent insecurity we feel over the consequences of our actions.

Anytime we are faced with an important decision, where the stakes are high, where we cannot be certain of the outcome, and where the consequences of making a poor choice may be catastrophic, we experience anxiety. That's a healthy sign; people who experience no anxiety at all under those circumstances usually turn out to be dangerous. In some of us, however, the anxiety doesn't know when to quit. It becomes like a software virus that replicates itself endlessly, until even the most trivial decisions and challenges of everyday life come to seem like insoluble problems. Chronic anxiety turns the journey of life into a treadmill of worry

12

and wasted effort, and once you find yourself on that treadmill, it's hard to get off.

This is where the phrase "have a little faith" would seem to apply, but if Godless Universe 4.0 is your operating system, your hard drive will reject most faith-based programs, and there are times when that can seem like a major disadvantage.

My parents had been raised as Baptists. Their parents were members of the same congregation, and that's where my mother and father first met as children. Apparently, the "good news" didn't make a lasting impression on the younger generation, however. By the time I was born, my parents were of one mind: They didn't want their own children to have anything to do with religion, organized or not. My siblings and I grew up learning more about Greek mythology than we did about Christianity, and we learned absolutely nothing about any of the world's other religions. I thought that churches were historical artifacts, like the Acropolis or the ruins of Machu Picchu, and it came as a real surprise to me to learn that many Americans—some of our neighbors, even!—actually believed what was preached in them.

I knew a few kids in school who attended something called catechism, but they seemed embarrassed by the whole thing and never spoke of it except to say that it was boring. I assumed it was like a Cub Scouts meeting, which I had tried once, and that was boring enough. None of my peers ever talked about religion, either in the classroom or on the playground, except to spread rumors that one boy in our grade, Alan Pitter, was Jewish. All that meant to me was that Alan's ancestors had worked on the pyramids, a fact that I'd learned not from reading the Bible but from watching Charlton Heston part the Red Sea.

When I finally did get old enough to ask questions about religion, my parents acknowledged that faith must serve a purpose, otherwise it wouldn't be so widespread and it wouldn't have been around for so long. For many people, it clearly provides reassurance in a dangerous, uncertain world. But faith only works if you believe in it; once doubt sets in, you have to start looking elsewhere for comfort. Art was where my parents looked for a sense of meaning and reassurance, and although the results were only fair to middling, I followed their example.

Five

WHEN I WAS A KID, my favorite character in *The Wizard of Oz* was the Cowardly Lion. I liked him because I could relate to his problems more easily than to any of the other characters' problems. I didn't live on a dreary farm, I could read at my grade level so I knew I had a brain, and I cried when I shot a bird with my BB gun, so I knew I had a heart. But the Lion, who hates himself for being afraid of his own shadow, won me over the moment he sang:

> I'm afraid there's no denyin'
> I'm just a dandy-lion
> A fate I don't deserve.

He hadn't *chosen* to be cowardly; it was the hand he was dealt, and he didn't like it one bit. He knew that there was something fundamentally unacceptable about being a lion with no self-confidence. He also knew that until he had straightened this problem out, he could never know peace; he could never feel at home in his own life. He would be a failure until he had proven—to himself and to everyone else—that if he ever met an elephant, he would wrap him up and sell-aphant. He had tried the positive-thinking approach: Act brave and you will become brave! Believe in yourself! Roar like you mean it! But we all know how that worked out. All it took was a slap on the nose from a little girl, and the illusion fell apart.

My mother stood less than five feet tall, and I started school when I was four, so I was always the shortest and youngest boy in my grade. I couldn't compete with any of the other boys in sports, my voice was as high as any of the girls', and beginning at age seven, I was a cellist in the school orchestra. (I chose the cello after my mother took me to hear Aldo Parisot give a recital, and I fell in love with the sight of the wood grain on the back of his instrument.) I was a little twerp, in other words, but I hadn't *chosen* to be a little twerp. It was the hand I was dealt, and I wanted a better one.

No amount of reassurance from my parents or viewings of *A Charlie Brown Christmas* could dissuade me from the belief that there was something fundamentally unacceptable about my low position in the pecking order. But if I wanted things to change, I knew it was up to me to do something about it. I couldn't pray for a growth spurt, and my parents couldn't make my voice change. I was a perfect candidate for conversion to a philosophy of humanistic self-determination, so it should come as no surprise when I tell you that in 1973, when I saw the character played by David Carradine on the television show *Kung Fu* for the first time, I felt the way the apostles must have felt when they first met Jesus.

Kwai Chang Caine, as portrayed by Mr. Carradine, was someone who had eradicated all traces of insecurity from his central nervous system. He'd also learned how to walk through walls, ignore pain, and kick pistols out of men's hands when the need arose. And he played the flute, if you can believe it. He was every little twerp's fantasy come to life.

He hadn't been born with all that wisdom and self-confidence. He'd acquired it at a place called the Shaolin temple, a Zen Buddhist monastery in northern China, and going there became my goal. The Shaolin temple wasn't accepting exchange students from American junior high schools that year, however, so I had to make do. I burned a lot of incense in the basement, wore a bald-head wig when I meditated so as to look like an authentic Buddhist monk, and walked barefoot to school every day, in the winter in Connecticut, to try to overcome pain. My mother heard about this and made me promise to wear shoes, and I did, but only after having cut the soles out of the bottoms. Be glad I wasn't your kid, that's all I can say.

I took kung fu lessons from the only teacher I could find in southwestern Connecticut, a man in need of anger-management counseling whose favorite maxim was "You can't walk in peace 'til you've walked through violence first." So as not to waste any time, he focused exclusively on the violence part.

His studio was a thirty-minute drive from our home. My parents took turns driving me, and sometimes my dad chose to stay during the lesson rather than to drive home. He sat in the waiting room and worked on needlepoint art to pass the time.

The master, exasperated by the lack of aggressive instinct I displayed when it came time to fight, gave me the nickname "candy-ass" and seemed to think that ridiculing me would cure me of my deficit. I convinced myself that his cruelty was some sort of test, an ordeal that he was putting me through in order to strengthen me and prepare me for the ultimate battle: the battle to conquer *myself*. So I sucked it up and let him humiliate me. In the meantime, I looked up Buddhism and Taoism in *The World Book Encyclopedia,* and this is the message that I took from there: Life sucks and then you die—unless you're enlightened. If you're enlightened, life sucks and then you die—*but that's OK.*

Enlightenment, apparently, is a highly evolved state of consciousness. If you can achieve it, all of your problems will be solved at once, in a blinding flash, and they will stay solved forever. From that moment on, no matter where you are or what happens to you, you will be at peace. Your mind will be cleared of impure, negative, painful thoughts. Your mind will be like a mirror, and your thoughts will be like images in that mirror that come and go freely, leaving no stain on its surface. Your false, painful identity as a selfish ego will be swept away, and your true identity as an expansive, accepting, compassionate Buddha will be revealed. You will become both desireless and fearless, and in doing so, you will become free of all suffering.

There was no mention of God in those entries, or any need for superhuman strength or wisdom. Suffering was an entirely man-made problem, and its solution could be achieved through human effort alone. All you had to do was meditate! To become enlightened, you didn't have to cram more facts and figures into your head. Quite the opposite—spiritual awakening was a process of clearing bothersome facts and figures away until there was only native, natural wisdom left. You had to let your mind relax and go quiet until it became as clear as the blue sky.

Hallelujah! My new philosophy gave me an ironclad excuse not to learn. I was sick of school anyway, so I told my parents that I had decided to become a Zen Buddhist. To help them understand my decision, I read them a passage from the *Tao Te Ching,* a sixth century BCE Taoist classic (not quite Buddhist, but close enough) that described the enlightened sages of old as follows:

Watchful, like men crossing a winter stream.
Alert, like men aware of danger.
Courteous, like visiting guests.
Yielding, like ice about to melt.
Simple, like uncarved blocks of wood.
Hollow, like caves.
Opaque, like muddy pools.

My mother couldn't find anything objectionable in this passage, so she gave me her blessing. My father nodded sadly and said, "My son, the block of wood. Let me know if it works."

I became obsessed with the goal of attaining enlightenment, and when I get obsessed with something, I do so in the clinical sense. I meditated on the school bus, in homeroom, during study hall and lunch, in the basement at home, in the backyard, on the couch in the living room, and in my bed. I even tried to meditate while I was watching TV. Whenever I caught myself *not* meditating, I pinched myself, stuck safety pins into my legs, or held matches near my arms. I hid the damage with long-sleeved shirts. There was no time to waste, the Buddha said. Work out your salvation with diligence.

Diligence was my specialty. Insecure teenagers tend to have lots of energy, and video games hadn't been invented yet, so I had few distractions. Unfortunately, when it comes to spiritual quests, it turns out that diligence can work against you. You have to extinguish your ego to become enlightened, it's true, but here's the paradox: Whenever you strive toward any goal, including the goal of extinguishing your ego, you end up giving your ego a workout. So the harder you try to become egoless, the more egotistical you become. Welcome to Paradox World, the theme park that you can never leave, because you carry it around with you!

The goal of attaining enlightenment through effort of any kind, when you get right down to it, is probably self-defeating. Yet for a lucky few, the effort leads to an indefinably satisfying experience. Just hang in there, the books said. Find a good teacher and do your best! Zen masters were in short supply in Ridgefield, Connecticut, in 1973, so for me it all boiled down to *Do your best.*

On paper, it sounds simple enough: Do your best. We hear that message every day of our lives. In this world, if you want something badly enough and are willing to push yourself to the limits of endurance and imagination to achieve it, you'll surely succeed. It may take a lifetime, but if you never give up, you'll cross the finish line someday. In actual practice, however, the goal of doing your best can turn out to be as unattainable as reaching the spot where a rainbow touches the ground. The goal always recedes; the gap between who you actually are and who you hope to become never seems to close.

Wise people adjust their expectations under these conditions. They stop comparing themselves to Buddha or Batman and trust themselves to achieve their personal best. Not me; I was not going to capitulate. Capitulation meant accepting that I might spend my whole life waiting for a better life to begin, and that was unacceptable. I was not going to be a quitter.

I dug in for the long haul. I stuck with the meditation and the kung fu all through junior high and then high school, where I received permission to study Chinese as an independent study project. The art teacher let me practice Chinese calligraphy on my own during his class, and the gym coaches let me practice kung fu in a corner of the basketball court rather than forcing me to shoot hoops or run track. A tenth-grade history teacher saw how passionate I was about all this, and he offered to help. He happened to be taking a graduate course in Chinese history at the time, so he shared all of his books with me and basically let me take the course with him. I was so deeply absorbed in my own little world, and so disconnected from the world my peers inhabited, that I doubt anyone noticed when I disappeared after my junior year. I applied to Yale University a year early and was accepted, but instead of matriculating right away, I took a year off and worked in an office mail room to save money for tuition.

At Yale, I majored in Chinese language and literature with a focus on the Buddhist and Taoist classics. I'd been reading those books in English translation for years, but the transformative miracle of enlightenment had not yet occurred. If I could read them in the original language, I thought, I might at last grasp their meaning directly.

Five years later, when I *could* read those books in the original language, I discovered that the translations I'd been reading were pretty accurate. Language wasn't the problem.

In 1982, I applied for a job to teach English at a medical college in mainland China for two years. When I got there, I made it my goal to study with as many kung fu masters as I could find. I stopped reading philosophy books and put all of my efforts into the physical challenge of learning as many traditional martial arts systems as possible. I thought of it as kung fu graduate school. I came back home ready to launch a career as a martial arts instructor, but then something unexpected happened. My back went out.

It didn't just go out once. It went out once every three months at first, then every other month, then every month, and when it went out, it was so bad that I could hardly move. Just breathing was exruciating, and getting up to use the bathroom became a twenty-minute ordeal. I consulted orthopedic surgeons, physical therapists, and acupuncturists. I tried yoga and biofeedback exercises, and I practiced tai chi every day, but nothing helped. On most days I couldn't even put my shoes on by myself. Needless to say, I knew there was something fundamentally unacceptable about being a martial arts guy who can't put on his own shoes.

And I hadn't become enlightened. Whenever my back went out, I became frustrated to the point of despair. Kwai Chang Caine wouldn't have let a bad back get to him; he would have seen it as an opportunity to be mindful of his posture. I had spent sixteen years trying to achieve peace of mind through Eastern spirituality, but instead of turning me into a block of wood, my efforts turned me into someone who might have been raised by Chinese rabbits.

In hindsight, I think I know why it didn't work. Here is a story from the *Zhuangzi*, a Taoist classic written in China around twenty-three centuries ago:

> If a man in a boat is crossing a river and an empty boat drifts along and bumps into his, he won't get angry. But if there is someone in the other boat, then the man will shout out directions to move. If his directions go unheeded, he will shout again, and then a third time, followed by a stream of curse words.

If a man could make himself empty, and pass like that through the world, then who could harm him?

It's a wonderful allegory, but it brings us right back to Paradox World: The harder you try to make yourself empty, the more full of yourself you become. If selflessness comes, it must come by some other means than one's own desire to be selfless. I ran out of steam before I could find out what those other means were. Instead, I discovered writing, and that gave me something new to think about for a while.

Six

WRITING IS AN IDEAL OCCUPATION if you're a rabbit. It gives you an excuse to stay in your burrow all day, and it allows you to explore problems like anguish and insecurity without having to solve them. You don't need to have peace of mind to be a writer; in fact, the more troubled you feel, the more you have to write about. For some writers (I consider myself a member of this group), writing doesn't happen as a result of ambition or self-discipline or love of literature. It happens for the same reason that a person who has an itch in the middle of his back will get up and find something to scratch it with: It is a means of relieving discomfort. The discomfort, in my case, happens to be the sort of emotional dissonance that an anxious mind projects onto the soundtrack of everyday experience.

Put on a pair of headphones, choose a tune that really gets on your nerves, and then listen to it while exercising, driving, or washing the dishes. If you're like me, you will find it an unpleasant experience. Now try doing the same thing while listening to the most beautiful piece of music you've ever heard. Feel better? That's what writers like me want to do: provide a coherent, pleasing soundtrack for the chaos swirling around us all. We want to make the human experience of freedom and responsibility seem less gratuitously dark, or at least to present the darkness in such a way that it seems less irredeemably hateful.

When it works, it feels great. When it doesn't work, and the dissonance goes unresolved in spite of all your efforts, it leaves you feeling hopeless. This, if you ask me, is the reason why so many writers self-destruct. If art can't relieve the discomfort, then what's left?

Here's how I became a writer. After I'd returned from China, friends and family encouraged me to write down some of the experiences I'd had there. I loved telling those stories, but it never occurred to me to write them down, because I'd never enjoyed writing. Writing had always felt more or less like a chore to me, a school assignment that had to be fulfilled so that a person could move on to the next level of school. Come to think of it, education in general often seemed to me to be like a giant spanking machine. You crawled your way through it simply to prove that you could make it through; at the end, you got your diploma and your life could finally begin.

In middle school and high school, I rarely read books unless I had to, or unless they contained information that I thought would bring me closer to my goal of enlightenment. My lack of interest in reading for pleasure gave way abruptly during the spring break of my sophomore year at college. Rather than go home for the two weeks, I decided to stay in the dorm by myself so that I could study Chinese day and night without any interruptions. After about a week of this Scrooge-like experiment, and after eating a lot of canned food warmed up on a hot plate, I started to feel lonely. In our dorm room, one of my roommates had installed a beanbag chair in the corner, and on that ugly, red lump sat a paperback book. The cover art showed a man wearing a World War II pilot's helmet, which appealed to me. Like most boys of my generation, I'd grown up building plastic and balsa-wood models of World War II airplanes and had always been fascinated by stories about World War II airmen, so I opened the book and decided to give it a try. The book was *The World According to Garp* by John Irving, and I didn't get up from that beanbag chair until I was half done with it.

When I did get up, I was angry. At the halfway point of the story, something terrible happens. This turn of events, which involved two children, was so upsetting to me that I slammed the book closed and stalked around the dormitory in a rage. I was furious at the author for planting that awful scene in my mind, and I cursed the fact that no matter how hard I tried, I couldn't remove it from my imagination. What sort of cruel, sick person would want to put readers through this? Why wasn't there a warning on the cover? This experience ruined my spring break. I couldn't study at all after that; I was haunted by that scene and by the tragic scenarios that unfolded in my head in its wake. I couldn't turn it off. And I threw that goddamned book in the garbage. I didn't care that it wasn't mine.

A month later, I went to a bookstore and bought another copy of that goddamned book. I just had to know how it ended, I couldn't stand not knowing any longer. I read the second half in another marathon session on the beanbag chair, and what a relief it was to get to the end. The author somehow resolved the terrible dissonance he'd created, and I got up from the chair feeling as if I had awakened into a new world, a world transfigured by horrifying beauty, by randomness, by mysterious order, by hate, by love, and by just about everything else. It was a confusing experience, but it was sublime. After that, I started reading for pleasure, and the authors I remember enjoying most during that time were Loren Eiseley, Willa Cather, E. B. White, Robertson Davies, and Frans G. Bengtsson.

Writing was another matter. Unlike reading, composition was slow and deliberate. Since the words were coming out of my own head, I never felt surprised by them. Because I rarely put more than the minimum required effort into what I wrote, the finished product brought me little satisfaction. But when I started writing about what had happened to me in China, I felt differently. These were stories that I enjoyed telling, so I had a basic confidence in the material. But the first few drafts I wrote came out awful. What was I doing wrong?

I discovered that writing a story isn't the same as telling it. Composition has its own requirements and its own set of rules. It bothered me that the stories didn't read well on the page. It became an itch that I had to scratch until the itch had gone away.

The painstaking ordeal of rewriting over and over again didn't feel like a chore anymore. It felt like a necessity. If you were cooking a roast for someone and could see that the meat was still frozen in the middle, you wouldn't serve it just because it was dinnertime. You'd keep that thing in the oven until it had thawed out and cooked. That's what you'd do, and that's how I felt about getting those first stories right. I didn't have to force myself to sit down and work on them; I felt pulled toward my desk and my ancient manual typewriter. And when, at last, I was satisfied with them, I felt as good as I'd ever felt when practicing martial arts—maybe even better. That's how writing saved me when my back gave out, and when those stories about China were published in 1987 under the title *Iron & Silk*—and received positive reviews and led to my being chosen as the subject of a Dewar's Scotch ad—that's when I decided that the life of a writer was the life for me.

Seven

I MET MY SOUL MATE the same year I started writing. A mutual friend introduced us, thinking we would have a lot in common because Jessica Yu was a fencer and fifth-generation Chinese-American. He invited us over for dinner at his apartment, and I took a liking to Jessica right away, in spite of the fact that she listened to punk rock, wore a pair of homemade earrings showing a cow being struck by a car, and topped it all off with a disheveled Mohawk. She had a dark sense of humor and a gift for storytelling, but most intriguing of all to me was the fact that she had clearly not been raised by rabbits. She was only nineteen years old but had the self-confidence and poise of someone decades older.

Unfortunately, my friend's inexperience as a matchmaker became evident when we learned that Jessica already had a boyfriend. This gave me an opportunity to demonstrate my persistence. Rabbits can't bust down doors, but they can gnaw through almost anything. I found out that Jessica, who was an undergraduate at Yale at the time, was taking a course in modern Chinese literature from a professor I knew. After waiting several months so as to avoid seeming obvious, I convinced the professor to let me visit the class as a guest lecturer to discuss life in contemporary mainland China. A few months later, I gave a demonstration of traditional Chinese sword techniques for the Yale fencing team. Then, exactly one year after that initial dinner, I heard from our mutual friend that Jessica and her boyfriend had split up. I called her right away and asked if she would join me for a drink to celebrate my birthday the following night. She sounded more perplexed than delighted but was too polite to say no.

At that time, I drove what I could afford, which was a rusted-out 1967 Volkswagen Bug that had a giant hole in the floorboards, no heat, and windshield wipers that didn't work. The night of our first date—my twenty-sixth birthday—the car wouldn't start after I'd dropped Jessica off at her apartment. I tried to jump-start it by pushing it down the street in the snow as fast as I could, hopping inside, and then popping the clutch. Twenty minutes later, one of her housemates glanced outside the window and asked, "Isn't that the guy you had dinner with?" They watched me until I'd pushed the car out of sight.

On our third date, during a freezing rain, the locks on the doors froze shut while we were having dinner. I had to borrow a lighter from someone in the restaurant and hold the flame under the door handles until the ice melted. Then I had to drive home with the window down so that I could keep the windshield clear by wiping it with my hand.

The biggest problem I faced, though, wasn't my crappy ride or my starving-artist lifestyle. It was having to overcome a cultural stereotype. White guys who have dedicated themselves to the study of Asian philosophy, language, and martial arts often come with baggage. If their attraction to traditional Asian culture is based on a combination of fantasy and misplaced idealism, they may be tempted to project versions of those fantasies onto contemporary Asian females, who have no interest in behaving like Tokugawa-era courtesans.

Jessica needn't have worried. Guys who fit that description tend to avoid Ivy League–educated athletes with nearly shaven heads who listen to Stiff Little Fingers and have pictures of Tommy

Hearns hung over their desks. And I had lived in China for two years, where the spectacle of brass-throated women berating their husbands in public—with delighted onlookers cheering them on—was a common occurrence. I had no misconceptions about Chinese women being submissive. Still, I understood what I was up against and figured, since I'd already waited a year, what was the rush? She kept me at arm's length for a while but eventually decided to give me a chance.

Our personalities complemented each other in ways that made for a lively but stable combination. The main thing, I think, is that because she had such deep reserves of self-confidence, she could enjoy my company without *needing* it—and she didn't expect or want me to need hers. Emotional drama wasn't her thing, and her untroubled presence made me feel less troubled myself.

We dated for two years before she graduated in 1987, then we moved to San Francisco, an hour's drive from where Jessica had been raised and where her parents still lived. The more time I got to spend with them, the more I liked them—and I'd liked them from the beginning. Her father, John, had been born in Shanghai and raised in the Philippines, where he experienced the horrors of war as a child during the Japanese occupation. He was an academic prodigy, which led to his enrollment at Stanford medical school at age nineteen. He chose oncology as his specialty and did his residency at Sloan-Kettering hospital in Manhattan, but instead of going into private practice, he joined the fledgling Kaiser hospital in Santa Clara in hopes of being part of a movement in the United States toward socialized medicine. Jessica's mother, Connie, was a fourth-generation Chinese-American whose father was a graduate of the Stanford School of Engineering who served as an officer of the U.S. Army during World War II. Connie became an antiwar activist during the Vietnam War, but her parents did not interfere with her choice and their relationship was preserved. Connie stayed home to raise the three children—Jennifer, Jessica, and their brother,

Marty—but still found time to become a published historian and a fencing coach.

Both John and Connie had been raised Catholic. During high school, John became very serious about religion and even considered joining the priesthood, but he chose medicine instead. Then, during the Vietnam War, when the Church refused to condemn America's role in that conflict, both he and Connie stopped attending services. As the war dragged on, they stopped believing in God. Jessica and her siblings, like me, were raised without religion.

The fact that I was not Chinese was never an issue for Jessica's parents. They'd campaigned for George McGovern, rooted for the 49ers before the team had won any Super Bowls, and named their only son after Martin Luther King—they were ethnic Californians, for heaven's sake. And besides, I could speak Chinese with Jessica's grandparents, all four of whom lived in the area. I was a shoo-in for the Promising Boyfriend role.

While I began work on a novel, Jessica launched her career as a filmmaker with a job arranging pasta on forks for a frozen foods commercial. We got married in a Japanese garden with Jessica's Uncle Al—a Chinese-American race car driver, how cool is that?—serving as our celebrant. And then, in 1989, we moved south to Los Angeles. We were young artists in love, we could beat anyone on our block in a sword or spear fight, and we owned a Toyota Corolla with windshield wipers that worked. What could go wrong?

Eight

I'LL TELL YOU WHAT COULD go wrong: She turned out to be more talented than me. I know, I know—your heart bleeds. Being married to a great talent is a problem most people would love to have, and it's a problem that I certainly do love having now, but before having children, and as each of my books seemed to take longer and longer to write and seemed to sell fewer and fewer copies, it was hard sometimes to look across the living room and watch her work—usually on several projects at once. She is to creativity what Old Faithful is to geysers: bountiful, inexhaustible, and . . . well, faithful. She delivers every day, rain or shine, on time and under budget. I, on the other hand, am more like a drain with roots growing in it: prone to restricted flow and aggravating blockages.

In 1996, she was nominated for an Academy Award for a short-subject documentary film she'd made called *Breathing Lessons: The Life and Work of Mark O'Brien*. It's about a writer who contracted polio as a child during the epidemic of the mid-1950s. The disease left him paralyzed from the neck down and unable to breathe on his own. He had to spend most of his life in a Jules Verne–ian contraption called an iron lung, with only his head protruding from one end of the vacuum chamber. After teaching himself to write by typing with a stick that he held in his mouth, he earned a degree from Berkeley and went on to publish regularly as a journalist and poet. Sandy Close, his editor and longtime friend, thought a film ought to be made about him, and she thought Jessica would be the right person to make it. She made the introductions and with Mark's blessing, Jessica produced, directed, and edited the film herself on a miniscule budget. In case you didn't watch the Oscars that year, I'll describe what happened.

"And the award goes to . . . *Breathing Lessons: The Life and Work of Mark O'Brien.* Director: Jessica Yu."

Jessica made her way to the stage while I craned my neck to see her over the top of Nicole Kidman's hairdo. Muhammad Ali and George Foreman were sitting together only a few rows away. I felt as if I had awakened to find myself in the hall of Valhalla, just in time to see my wife shed her mortal form and take her place in the firmament. Jessica accepted the statue from Will Smith and Tommy Lee Jones and then said to nearly a billion viewers around the world, "You know you've entered new territory when you realize that your outfit cost more than your film."

I've been asked many times if that line was true. The answer is yes, but with an asterisk. The outfit cost *us* nothing. The dress was a loaner from a designer, the diamond jewelry borrowed from Harry Winston in Beverly Hills. The *value* of the outfit, however, did exceed the total production cost of her film by a margin of four to one.

Immediately following the program, the nominees and their guests moved to a large banquet hall adjacent to the theater for the Governors Ball, the Academy's official celebration. The room was crammed with movie stars and their entourages. Jessica's parents sat with us at our table, and they were ecstatic. Connie, my mother-in-law, said that when Jessica got up on stage and the monitors overhead showed us what television viewers all over the world were seeing, she felt overcome by emotion. She suddenly remembered being a little Chinese-American girl in San Francisco, watching the Oscars with her parents on a black-and-white television set in the 1950s. None of the faces that appeared on the screen ever looked like hers or any of her relatives'. Celebrities didn't have single-fold eyelids in those days. Now look whose face was on the screen! Her own daughter's.

Just as the dinner entrée was served, a publicist for the event came to fetch Jessica and lead her around the room to be photographed with the other award winners. "It's for the archives," she explained. "You won't need your purse, Ms. Yu—just bring the Oscar."

Jessica's parents weren't going to miss this. They went with her, while I got the assignment of staying at the table and watching her purse. The other people at our table had after-parties to attend, so they took off a few minutes later. It was just me and the floral centerpiece.

Husbands who have had to watch their wives' purses agree that it is a challenging task. How do you convey to strangers that the purse belongs in your care—you aren't stealing it—yet it is definitely not yours? The trick, I think, is to manage to look both aggrieved and nonchalant at the same time. I stuck the purse on the empty seat next to me, stared at my dessert fork, and pretended to be glad of the chance to have a quiet moment to myself. This was fine for forty minutes or so, but when I had to use the bathroom, my anxiety peaked. Here I was, in the same room as Muhammad Ali and George Foreman, and I was about to pass by their tables holding a purse. A small, sparkly purse. And this was before BlackBerrys, cell phones, and other personal electronic devices had come along, when men never carried anything in public.

I held it away from my body with my thumb and index finger. I intended to look purposeful, like someone who had spotted the object on the ground and was bringing it to the lost-and-found desk. I hurried past the manly role models of my youth and found, to my relief, that the men's room was empty. But before I could finish, the door opened behind me and Al Pacino—who had presented the Best Picture award that night—stepped inside. He glanced at me, then at the purse, and then he moved as far away from me as he could, to the farthest stall. After washing my hands, I stuffed the purse under my coat jacket and held it under my armpit, and that's where it stayed until the Governors Ball ended.

On our way home that night, Jessica took off the Harry Winston bracelet and held it up under our car's overhead light while I drove. The diamonds cast glittering, rainbow-hued images all over the interior of the car. We teased each other about the fact that there was something Cinderella-ish about the way the night had ended: The jewelry and dress had to be returned, we were taking our desserts home in a doggie bag (chocolate Oscar statues dipped in gold flake), and our car—the Toyota Corolla, by then nine years old—had indeed resembled a pumpkin coach when the valet attendants brought it up for us. The actor Red Buttons and a group of his friends had been chatting with us on the curb, congratulating Jessica on her brilliant acceptance speech, when our dust-streaked sedan pulled up between a stretch limo and a town car.

The spell was broken, but we still had the Oscar with us and an outfit that was worth more than our house. Jessica held the bracelet right up close to her eyes and looked through the diamonds. "You've got to try this!" she gasped. She took control of the steering wheel for me so I could have a peek, and against the night sky the vision was truly spectacular—I felt as if I were floating inside the heart of a star cluster.

Just as we merged onto the 134 Freeway, I heard Jessica say, "Uh-oh." She was staring very closely at the bracelet now and frowning. "One of the diamonds is missing."

Oh my god, I thought. *Oh my god.*

She searched through the folds of her dress but couldn't find it. "Oh well," she said, "I'm sure it will turn up."

When we got home, we saw that some friends had plastered the front of our house with homemade banners and showered the driveway with confetti. We went inside, relived the high points of our magical evening, and then went to bed. I couldn't stop thinking about the bracelet. What would happen the next morning, when we drove to Beverly Hills to return it?

I tossed and turned until I couldn't stand it any longer. I got up, grabbed a flashlight, and went out to the garage. I looked under the floor mats of the car, under all of the seats, everywhere. I checked the driveway for anything that sparkled—the confetti slowed my progress—and then, back inside the house, I got down on my hands and knees and searched the floor. I looked everywhere Jessica might have passed once she'd gotten dressed, but no diamond turned up.

I went back to bed and lay there, imagining the scene that would take place on Rodeo Drive in just a few hours. I rehearsed what I would say to the manager and how I would say it. I would convey to him how seriously we took the matter, that I'd been up all night searching for the diamond, that we weren't scammers or slobs. I pictured the look on the manager's face, and of course, his expression would reveal what he was too refined a man to say out loud: He suspected us of pulling the diamond out as a souvenir. We weren't famous movie stars who could buy their own diamonds, after all—we were "emerging artists," which is a polite way of saying we were broke. We ate microwavable frozen dinners to save money, we bought our clothes at Target, and we drove a nine-year-old car. I imagined the manager recommending that we check our homeowner's insurance—if we had any, that is—to see if it might cover the loss.

As dawn broke, my anxiety turned to paranoia. What if this was a scam that someone at Harry Winston's was running? An employee could easily pull out a diamond, guessing that people like us would be too excited to notice it right away, and that we would be too ashamed to refuse to accept responsibility for its loss. The store would be reimbursed and the employee would keep the diamond. The more I thought about this, the more agitated I got. As soon as Jessica woke up, I told her that I wanted to get this over with right away. She assured me that the matter would be settled amicably, but nothing she said could relieve the tension in my mind and in my lower back, which had locked up like a vise. We drove to Beverly Hills, and when we arrived, a very large security guard opened the front door for us and led us to the manager, who looked and sounded exactly as he'd looked and sounded in my imagination. His black hair, glistening with product, was as shiny as his Italian leather shoes. If you'd turned the man upside down, you would hardly have noticed the difference. Jessica showed him the bracelet and pointed out the empty setting. My nemesis nodded and said, "Let me check the box; it might be there." His shoes made a disagreeable tapping sound as he walked across the marble floor to the back room. He returned a few minutes later with a shallow container. "Yes, it's right here. It happens sometimes with the newer pieces; the settings have to be adjusted."

When we got home later that morning, more than a dozen floral arrangements—all of them huge—sat waiting for us on the doorstep. And they were only the first to arrive. By the end of the day, I felt as if we were living inside one of the Rose Bowl parade floats. The phone rang continually—Jessica received congratulatory calls from relatives, colleagues, and friends she hadn't seen since preschool. "Don't bother answering the phone," she said to me when she had to go out. "Let the machine take care of it." I followed her advice and listened as ten different callers left messages in the space of fifteen minutes. The eleventh caller had just identified himself as an agent, when the tape in our primitive answering machine ran out. I lurched to the phone and picked it up.

"Hello?" I said.

"Jessica Yu, please."

I told the agent that she was in a meeting and offered to take a message.

"Am I speaking to her assistant?"

I smiled. "No, I'm her husband."

"Ah, Mr. Yu—congratulations! I hear you're a writer."

Nine

THE YEAR JESSICA RECEIVED THE OSCAR, I was struggling to complete a novel about a Carmelite nun with epilepsy, and I was deeply stuck. In all of my novels, I end up creating fictional characters who are tormented by the gap between who they actually are and who they had hoped to become. They think it is up to them to bridge that gap, *to become who they choose to be,* and they fail. They are anxious, disappointed idealists who seem unable to take life as it comes—when we first meet them, that is. By the end of the novels, however, they have found some way to loosen their grips on their ideals, embrace reality, and become less rabbit-like.

I resent the implication, by the way—occasionally found in reviews of my work—that I use writing as a means of coming to terms with my own problems. The fact that I use writing as a means of coming to terms with my own problems is so obvious that implying it amounts to a form of passive-aggressive griping, like *implying* that soldiers resort to violence as a means of resolving conflict. If a reviewer really wanted to out me, what he or she would say is: "Mark Salzman uses writing as a means of coming to terms with his own problems, but he's been at it for a long time and is still writing about the same problems, so he must not be making much progress."

Touché!

My Carmelite nun had entered the cloister because she longed for the peace that surpasseth understanding. After decades of fruitless searching, she begins having mystical experiences, and these do bring her a kind of peace, but they are accompanied by increasingly severe headaches. Eventually, a doctor tells her that she has a form of epilepsy that may be the cause of her mystical experiences. She begins to doubt the authenticity of those experiences, and her peace of mind vanishes as she struggles with the decision whether or not to have the epilepsy treated.

It's my kind of story, all right, but somewhere along the way it occurred to me that a story about a nun with epilepsy might not appeal to readers any more than, say, a story about a failed cellist, which just happened to be the subject of another novel that didn't make the bestseller list and that just happened to have been written by me. My novels, I reasoned, are too *niche-y* to attract a wide audience. They are about weirdos with weird problems leading weird lives. They read as if they were written by a guy who wore a bald-head wig and cut the soles out of the bottoms of his shoes.

I became determined to find a way to make the nun's story more appealing. To accomplish this feat, I decided to have her fall in love with her neurologist.

As soon as I began imagining the doctor in his white lab coat and the nun in her modest, brown habit, both of them struggling for words to express their feelings for each other in a dark hospital at night, I realized that the story had major-motion-picture potential. I figured some Hollywood wunderkind with a baseball cap, wire-rimmed glasses, and a beard could turn it into a cross between *Witness* and *Awakenings,* and we'd all benefit. I got very excited about this idea and spent the next five years trying to write the book, but I couldn't get my stand-ins for Harrison Ford and Kelly McGillis to act like real people. They lurched through every scene like a pair of cardboard cutouts. By the third year, I was so frustrated that even the slightest sound distracted me as I wrote, so I took to wearing a huge towel wrapped around my head and a pair of busted stereo headphones on top of the towel to block out all unwanted noise. This solved the sound problem, but we had two cats at the time—one white and one brown, named Fog and Smog—and they liked to sit on my lap when I worked, which also distracted me. Cats don't like tinfoil, so I fashioned a tinfoil skirt that I wore along with the towel and the earphones to help me concentrate. These mechanical aids failed to cure my writer's block, but they did give our gas meter reader something to think about when he caught a glimpse of me through the window. In desperation, I moved to the one place where I felt so trapped that the only way I could get out was through writing, and that was the passenger seat of my car. Every morning, I pulled the car out of the garage, parked it under a tree in our driveway, and then hopped over the emergency brake into the passenger seat. It was quiet, and the cats couldn't get in there, but Fog, still angry over the tinfoil skirt, padded every day up the hood and windshield and sat down right on the moonroof. The view from where I sat served as the perfect metaphor for what I was going through: I was staring up a cat's ass.

I wrote draft after draft, but each turned out to be worse than the last. I got fed up with the characters and the plot, but most of all, I got fed up with me. Writers are not just the authors of their stories, after all; we are supposed to be the authors of our own lives, like everyone else, and I was creating a bad life. A lot more was at stake than just the book. When you are writing, more is always at stake than just the book.

What makes a life successful? I've always thought it boiled down to wisdom and effort—but mainly effort. You succeed when you make the right choices and muster up sufficient effort to do what you want to do, learn what you want to learn, and become what you want to become. What is always at stake when you set out to do something important is your integrity, which I define as how you measure up in terms of accepting responsibility for your own destiny—and then not screwing it up.

Each of us allegedly possesses the gift of will, the power to choose what to do and then to go out and do it. With every bad choice we make, and every failure to apply sufficient effort to fulfill our goals, we squander that gift. We are supposed to make *navigation* our means of conveyance through our life journeys—as opposed to drifting around like coconuts that have gotten washed out to sea.

The only way to get myself out of the mess I'd created, I decided, was through greater effort. I couldn't become smarter or more talented, but I could certainly whip myself harder. So I did what comes naturally to rabbit-people in these situations: I terrified myself with scenarios of failure. If I couldn't get this novel written, I thought, it meant that I was all washed up. Suck it up!

I trudged forward with all the enthusiasm of a participant in a forced march. I thought I had a breakthrough when, toward the end of year five, I concluded that the contrived romance between the nun and the neurologist was the problem. I wrote a draft without it, focusing entirely on the nun's struggle to decide whether to get the operation or not, and when it was finished I felt vindicated. I had passed my own test; I had discovered what writing is really about; I was an artist after all. I sent it off to my editor, feeling sure that she would love it. When she didn't love it, I was crushed.

That's when Jessica, the supreme problem solver, took charge. She wanted her relatively cheerful husband and the passenger seat of our car back. "You need a change of scenery," she said. She encouraged me to apply for a residency at the MacDowell Colony, an artists' retreat in the woods of New Hampshire, and I took her advice. When I was offered a residency there, Jessica made sure I got on the plane. I arrived at the end of September, just as the leaves were beginning to turn, and the first thing I carried into my secluded cabin in the woods was a container of boxed wine. I set myself up on a rocking chair on the porch with the wine right next to me, and I didn't bother to get up out of that chair except to eat and sleep for the next five days. I had no idea what I was doing, or what I was going to do with my time there, but the surroundings were so gorgeous I couldn't help but give in to it all and enjoy the view. On the sixth day, feeling more relaxed than I had in a long time, I stepped into the colony's main office to drop off a postcard. A member of the staff greeted me and asked how I was enjoying my residency so far. Suddenly feeling embarrassed about the loafing and the Wine-in-a-Box, I said that I was sure I would get lots of writing done before my six weeks were up. She smiled patiently—she probably heard the same thing all the time from writers who were just getting up from their third nap of the day—and said, "If that happens, great. But please don't feel that you've wasted your time here if it doesn't. What some artists need most is a chance to slow down for a while. If that's all you do here, don't worry, we won't report you to the National Endowment for the Arts."

My feet barely touched the ground as I walked out of that office. Someone was giving me permission to not write! I felt like a farmer being paid to not grow corn.

After that, everything at that colony felt like a gift: the fall colors, the sounds, the little homemade cookies in the picnic baskets that the staff brought to the cabins. But the biggest gift of all was the removal of all reminders of art as a profession, as a way of making money or gaining a reputation, and even as a means of solving one's own existential problems through the resolution of fictional ones. Everyone there wanted the same thing: to be reminded of what it felt like to be pulled toward his or her work, and to be unable to resist.

I decided not to think about the novel at all. I surrendered unconditionally and turned my residency into a vacation. Years' worth of accumulated tension melted away, and in its place came a feeling of euphoria, and in that euphoric state I suddenly found myself wanting to rewrite the novel. I knew how I wanted it to end now: I wanted the main character to be humbled until she was reminded of why she'd entered the cloister in the first place. She'd gone there to find the sacred in the ordinary, to seek God in this imperfect life of ours rather than outside of it, but she'd lost sight of that goal over time. Instead, she'd convinced herself that experiences of the sacred must be extraordinary, so nothing short of extraordinary experiences could satisfy her longing. I wanted her to be reminded of what it felt like to be faithful rather than determined, accepting rather than expectant. I wanted her, in other words, to have the experience I was having at the colony.

My editor accepted the draft I wrote in the cabin, and Jessica got her relatively cheerful husband and her car seat back. But the biggest surprise of all came about a month after I'd finished the book, when I had an unoriginal—yet deeply affecting—insight into the relationship between conscious will and creativity.

If the prospect of having to hear someone's unoriginal insight about the relationship between conscious will and creativity makes you cringe, don't worry; I'll make it fast. Here it is: The perceived relationship between conscious will and creativity is some sort of illusion. There is no direct relationship there; you can't make the Muse sing. There is no muscle you can squeeze in order to produce better ideas or come up with good ideas faster. Thinking otherwise leads to all sorts of unnecessary strain and the wearing of embarrassing outfits.

This realization made me feel so uncharacteristically relaxed that when, later that year, Jessica looked at me over dinner one night and said, with no more force than you would use to blow out a candle, "Let's start a family," I said, "OK"—completely forgetting that only a year earlier, and for at least a dozen years before that, I told anyone who would listen that having children would be the end of me.

It would be, I had insisted, like throwing a drowning man a life vest made out of concrete. Neither of my siblings had children, so I didn't have any nieces or nephews to bounce on my knee until my paternal instinct kicked in. Here's a short list of the reasons I thought it would be better if the buck stopped here: birth defects, contagious diseases, disfiguring accidents, poverty, war, mental illness, compulsory education, social rejection, environmental collapse, injustice, and just plain bad luck. I had nothing against babies—they're certainly cute enough—but when I looked at them, I would usually think: *You poor thing. Maybe you'll be one of the lucky ones, but chances are you're looking at seventy or eighty years of drawn-out suffering, occasionally interrupted by moments of pleasure.*

Cosmologists say that the universe is fifteen billion years old. That's a long time. Do any of us have painful memories of what it was like to be a hydrogen atom in the center of a star or a carbon atom floating in empty space or a water molecule inside the body of a dinosaur? No. For all of those eons of time, there were no problems, there were no tragedies, and there was no possibility of betrayal or disappointment. There was only existence, a web of matter and energy and space and time, full of possibility but empty of significance.

For there is nothing either good or bad, but thinking makes it so.

Hamlet's words, not mine. You don't have to be an overwrought Danish prince to conclude that existence without human consciousness sounds humane. It's the gift you give to the child you don't have, and that's the gift I wanted to bestow.

Jessica saw this issue differently. Her list of reasons in favor of passing the buck along would include: biological imperative (i.e., it's what living organisms do; get used to it), wonder, curiosity, knowledge, surprise, discovery, love, friendship, food, art, books, music, movies, medicine, and an excuse to go trick-or-treating again. But she, as I mentioned before, is someone for whom anxiety and depression have never been problems. She could never understand the real reason I was afraid to become a father: If a child of mine were to look at me one day with her face twisted in anguish or grief or terror and cry out, "Why won't my mind stop hurting?" I would never be able to forgive myself for the part I'd played in making that nightmare real.

After my catharsis in New Hampshire, however, my soundtrack music had changed. At age forty, I felt relaxed rather than anxious. Instead of dissonance I sensed harmony, and the harmony seemed to permeate everything.

There was another reason for my change of heart. In 1997, I had begun teaching writing as a volunteer at Central Juvenile Hall, where the most violent underage criminals in Los Angeles were sent to await trial and sentencing. I was invited to that hellish place to visit a creative writing class taught by a friend of mine, and my understanding was that the visit was to be a one-time-only deal. I'd never been to a lockup facility before, and the moment I got there, I wished I could be somewhere else. But what I saw and heard in the storage room where the class met took me by surprise, and before I knew it, I had agreed to start my own class there. My students were boys aged fifteen to seventeen, and most of them were facing murder charges. They had been dealt far worse hands than I had in life. Unlike me, they had substantial, real-life reasons to feel insecure, beginning with the fact that most of them had done things before being old enough to drive that would keep them in prison for the rest of their lives. They were frightened, angry, wounded, confused, self-hating, other-hating, and most of all lonely, but when they wrote about their wrecked lives and read their work aloud to each other, their loneliness subsided, even if only briefly. The intensity of their need for attention and encouragement, especially from adult males, was overwhelming, and I was an adult male who wasn't obliged to help carry out their punishments. That was being taken care of by professionals. I was a writer who enjoyed reading what they wrote, and I encouraged them to write more; it was that simple. During the time we spent together, their guilt or innocence became irrelevant. Only writing mattered, and I didn't have to pretend to appreciate the things they shared with me, which were their deepest concerns. Their suffering was painful to witness, but if the mere presence of a sympathetic teacher could relieve some of that suffering, it made me think: *The presence of a sympathetic parent would be even better.* Maybe, after all, I *would* know what to do if a child of my own were suffering, and who can say what, in the final tally, the real value of my child's experience in this world would be? I'd met parents whose children had suffered, but I'd never heard them say they wished their child had never been born.

"OK," I said to Jessica, and on only two conditions: I didn't want to change diapers, and I wanted to rent an office outside the home so I could work there five days a week. I could almost see myself in the old-fashioned dad role—coming home from work at dinnertime, reading to the kids before bed, taking them to the park on weekends—but I could not see myself as a modern, *involved* dad. I'd seen those guys at the farmers' market with diaper bags slung over their shoulders and defeated expressions on their faces, and it just didn't look right.

Jessica agreed to these terms, and nine months later (on time and under budget, that's how Jessica works) a delivery room nurse handed our daughter to me, and when the baby's tiny hand closed around one of my fingers and squeezed, I changed my mind about the diapers. And I never mentioned getting an office outside of the house again.

If anguish is like a software virus, then the feeling you get when you hold your own baby for the first time is like a software vaccine. It's self-replicating, and it spreads through your mind faster than the speed of thought, but instead of making you feel sick, it makes you believe you will never feel sick again. It makes you feel immortal. Not in the clichéd sense of *I will live on through my child!* That's for amateurs. I'm talking about a feeling of protectiveness, love, awe, purpose, and delight so intense that it overwhelms not only your sense of yourself or your surroundings but even your sense of time. This, surely, is what is meant by the phrase *the eternal present.* Maybe only a person who had turned the thought of having children into a decades-long arm-wrestling match with himself could feel the mixture of astonishment and humility I felt when I experienced that feeling for the first time.

Our first night in the hospital, after baby Ava had nursed at around five in the morning, I took her so that Jessica could get a few minutes of sleep. I put the baby, swaddled tightly in her blanket, next to me on the foldaway bed and lay there in the darkness on my side, with one hand cradled around her so she couldn't roll away and fall on the floor and break like an egg. The sky outside our window began to get light. I stared at Ava's sleeping face and here, more or less, are the words that passed through my mind at that moment: *I cannot believe that I just spent forty-one years worrying about insignificant bullshit like being short or having a bad back or writing niche-y novels, when the obvious reason that I exist at all is to be lying here right now, making sure that this knit cap doesn't slide off our baby's head. She could catch cold!*

Not everyone enjoys taking care of infants—some parents can hardly wait until their children can think and talk and begin to differentiate between self and other. I, on the other hand, hoped Ava would never grow up. In my eyes, the fact that she didn't yet know what words meant, and had no concept of herself as something distinct from anything else, made her the greatest show on earth. She was conscious, but her consciousness was as clear as a pond on a windless day. It was all awareness without any ideas churning inside it or blowing across its surface. Her mind was a work of nature, not yet of culture, and the thing about works of nature is that they can seem perfectly still even when they are moving. Being around her stilled my own mind in a way that deliberate exercises like meditation never could; the sight of her shone so brightly in my mind that ideas and inner conflict all got lost in the glare.

Quiet can mean a lot more than the absence of sound. Imagine that you are in a concert hall, in your seat, waiting for the program to begin. You had to fight through traffic for over an hour to get there. You had a long, hard day even before making that drive. The hall is filled with the sound of the audience as friends greet each other, couples chat, and ushers guide latecomers to their seats. One man is laughing way too loudly; a woman is coughing; some jerk is talking on his cell phone. Their voices bother you; the sound almost hurts your ears. Then the lights dim, and the featured performer walks on stage. He takes his seat at his instrument, makes a few adjustments, and then goes still. The audience does the same and becomes completely silent. This silence isn't empty; it is so rich with anticipation and wakefulness and joy that you feel as if your heart might burst. That is what I heard and felt whenever I held my pre-verbal child, so I found reasons to hold her a lot.

Diapers, bottle feedings, burping, baths, dressing, tickling, tummy time, singing, reading aloud, stroller walks, park visits, checkups, driving around at midnight because the movement of the car put her to sleep—anything that didn't require nipples, I did it, and it was the best job I ever had. No book or class could have prepared me for this, nor could I have imagined the transformation that occurred in terms of my everyday habits and routines, right down to the tiniest detail. The moment the baby was born, everything changed, except the fact that I had to breathe. All of a sudden, Jessica and I were busier than we had ever been in our lives, performing a seemingly endless array of tasks that neither of us had ever performed before—and purchasing, assembling, and disinfecting equipment that we had never even heard of. We learned to examine every object and surface around us for signs of potential danger; we worried about the baby's jaundice and umbilical hernia and the v-shaped birthmark on her forehead; we realized, with a baby in the car, that driving on any freeway in Los Angeles is about as smart as playing Russian roulette; and we did our best to adjust to a schedule that only astronauts preparing to descend to the moon's surface might recognize.

Our emotions were amplified to their limits. We were in a state of high alert, euphoria, and exhaustion all rolled into one. And so much was happening all at once! One morning, when Ava was about two weeks old and I was so sleep-deprived that I couldn't remember my own name, I was making oatmeal, when suddenly the baby started crying and the phone rang at the exact same time. I rushed over to pick up the baby first, then grabbed the phone with my free hand. It was my mother, calling to check in. As I was speaking to her, I heard an ominous noise. The pot of oatmeal was boiling over. Instinctively, I rushed over to get the pot off the stove. At that moment, Jessica appeared in the kitchen, saw me with the baby in my left arm and a pot of scalding water in the other, and shrieked, "What are you DOING?" and yanked the child out of my arms. I felt so ashamed that I nearly poured the oatmeal over my own head to show remorse.

Then, five minutes later, Jessica and I were on the couch listening to Ava make bubbling sounds with her mouth, and all was forgiven.

They say that the best way to learn a foreign language is to enroll in an immersion course. The idea is to place yourself in an environment where only the new language is spoken and heard, day in and day out. It's confusing and exhausting, but it works. Taking care of an infant is an immersion experience. Almost no aspect of your former life remains intact: You cannot read even a newspaper article without being interrupted, much less a book. You cannot finish a sentence when you are talking to your spouse. You cannot sleep for more than forty-five minutes at a time. Your center of gravity shifts from the area in your chest where your heart lies to the midpoint between your child's heart and your own. You dissolve, whether you like it or not.

Ten

I DIDN'T EVEN TRY TO WRITE during that first month of parenthood. Then I did try, during Ava's naps, but it didn't go well. Just before Ava was born, I had started a book about teaching at juvenile hall, but when I tried to pick up where I'd left off, I found that I couldn't concentrate for more than a few minutes at a time. But I didn't mind—I had a baby, for goodness' sake; I had a perfectly good excuse for not writing. After my experience in New Hampshire, I'd learned my lesson: When I try to force myself to write out of a sense of duty or fear, nothing comes out. Meanwhile, Jessica wanted to nurse Ava for at least a year but couldn't afford to withdraw completely from professional life, so when she started working again, I followed her around on film and television sets and to film festivals—baby in one arm and diaper bag in the other—where I shared gossip with the nannies-to-the-stars and read a lot of Little Golden Books aloud in trailers, hotel rooms, and airports. I became a modern, *involved* dad.

Physicists claim that more happened, in terms of interactions between fundamental particles, in the first second following the Big Bang than has happened in the fifteen billion years since—something to do with time and space being compressed. Same with having a baby. It feels as if more happens to you in that first year than has happened in your whole life up until then and probably will ever happen after that first year ends. Then you come out of it, and you start to decompress, but you've been changed. You have an impressive set of new skills, but most of them have already become obsolete (assembling the travel crib, mixing formula, anchoring the infant car seat, disinfecting the breast pump components without melting them) and many of your old, prechild life skills have deteriorated. Meanwhile, your child is beginning to talk and think and invent. She's not just a helpless animal anymore; she's a little person.

At this point, what you would most like would be for everything to slow down for a while, just to give you time to catch up. Instead, when you emerge from the infant-care compression chamber, you find yourself with a toddler on your hands, and then life hits you with all of the stuff you've been ignoring or putting off for the last year, and it all seems to demand your attention at once.

After Ava's first birthday, Jessica pointed out that if we were going to move to a district with a good public school system, we had better not wait until the last minute. We began visiting neighborhoods and attending open houses, but before we could put our old house on the market, my father called from Tucson to say that he had news for us. "I'm afraid it's not good," he said. Then he put my mother on the phone.

"We just came from the doctor's office," she said. "I have lung cancer."

Jessica, Ava, and I flew out to Tucson that weekend. My mother was still waiting for the report from her CT scan, so everyone was feeling anxious. This is where having a baby comes in handy. Ava was the miracle child; she entertained my parents for the whole weekend. We flew home on a Monday, and that Thursday, Mom called again with the results of her scan. The cancer was inoperable and could not be irradiated. Her prognosis: six to eighteen months of life.

Jessica was away on a job, so I took Ava with me to Tucson the next day. That night, after Mom had anesthetized herself with a few gin and tonics and then staggered upstairs to bed, my father and I were sitting in the kitchen, unable to think of a word to say, while Ava sat in a corner and "read" one of her board books aloud. My father suddenly stood up, went to the freezer, and took out a pint of ice cream. He put some of it on a spoon and said, "Ava's going to walk tonight." He got her attention and held out the spoon toward her. "Come on, Ava. Walk." Ava was able to stand at that point, but had not taken any steps yet. She took one look at the ice cream on that spoon, closed her book, stood up, and then walked across the kitchen to get it. "That's my girl," my father said. He had tears in his eyes.

A week after that visit, we got another call. This time it was from Connie, my mother-in-law. My father-in-law, who had retired only a year before, had just had a stroke. His left arm, left leg, and the left side of his face had been affected, but he could still walk. He could understand what you said to him but couldn't read or write, and when he tried to speak, the words came out all scrambled. Connie insisted that we not fly up to San Francisco to see them, because she knew how much travel we'd just done flying back and forth to Tucson. Instead, she and John flew down to visit *us* only a week after his stroke. When I met John at the airport, he smiled and said, "When I preach the door, everything that is up where coffee is dog letter." I had not yet been able to cry over my mother's news, but when I heard those words come out of my father-in-law's mouth, I choked up and had to turn away.

Jessica and I put our moving plans on hold. Instead, she came up with a bold idea: We would take all four of our parents to Italy. My mother had visited there once to give a recital in Florence and had often said she'd like to return. And Jessica's parents had taken all three of their kids to Italy twenty-five years earlier and had loved it. Jessica convinced her sister Jennifer, my brother Erich, and my sister, Rachel, to join us, along with Rachel's husband, Daniel, and their one-year-old daughter, Isabela. We had a terminal cancer patient, a stroke victim, two toddlers, and a pair of single thirty-somethings in our caravan, and somehow it all worked.

My mother savored that trip down to the last bite of pasta. Every meal she had there, she said, was the best meal she'd ever eaten in her life. John was recovering steadily and could already speak in short sentences. Another benefit of that journey was that I got to spend some time with my siblings. They both lived in Connecticut, where we'd grown up, and in the fifteen years since I'd moved west I'd probably seen them only three or four times. I talked to Erich on the phone fairly often, but Rachel and I only called each other on Thanksgiving, Christmas, and our birthdays. She and I were four years apart, and I'd left home for college when she was only thirteen. Then I went to China for two years, and then I'd moved to California. We loved each other, but in truth, we hardly knew each other as adults.

She'd married a human dynamo, a Romanian immigrant who escaped from that country during the dark years of the Ceausescu regime. Once he got to this country, Daniel learned how to install tiles and had a clear goal in mind: He wanted to *own* the company he worked for. He showed up one day in 1994 at Rachel and Erich's shop, showed them photographs of his work, and got himself hired on the spot. After a few months, when he had shown them what he could do, he made them an offer they couldn't refuse: "I don't want to be an employee of this company," he said. "I want to be one of its owners. Make me a partner and you won't regret it."

Daniel was optimistic, confident, and had real-life skills—what Salzman can resist that combination? Erich and Rachel were both won over, but Rachel took it to another level: She fell in love with him. They were married in 1998, and Isabela, their first child, was born two years later.

Having children finally gave my sister and me something to talk about. Our first opportunity to see each other's kids came in

October 2001, just a few weeks after the 9/11 attacks. Jessica had to travel to New York City for a job, and she didn't want to be separated from Ava, who was only five months old at the time, so the three of us made the trip together. During our visit, Rachel drove down from Connecticut with Isabela to have lunch with Ava and me. We picked up some food at a deli and took our strollers and diaper bags out to Central Park for a picnic.

Rachel and I watched Isabela chase butterflies while Ava napped in her stroller. The ruins of the World Trade Center were still burning only a few miles away, but we didn't want to think about the end of the world that day. Instead, we talked about onesies and sleep aids and diaper malfunctions. At one point she said, "Since having a baby, I don't feel so guilty about not making art anymore. It's a big relief, actually." She made a sweeping gesture with her arm, as if clearing a stack of unpaid bills off a desk in front of her, and then she tossed her head back and laughed.

In Italy we got to talk some more. By then, Ava and Isabela were old enough that they could play together. We'd brought along Ava's collection of Little Golden Books, and Rachel and I took turns sharing a pair of reading glasses (these books aren't called "little" for nothing) and reading them aloud to the girls. One night in Lucca, after watching our mother struggle to climb the flight of stairs to her bedroom, gasping for breath on every step, Rachel sighed and buried her face in her hands. "I feel really ashamed to say this, Mark," she said, "but I'm really glad I have Isabela right now. It gives me a reason not to think about Mom."

I told her that I felt the same way. That was the secret we shared on that trip. We agreed that parenthood had made us both feel that the human condition was more fragile and more terrifying than either of us had imagined, but also more beautiful.

When our mother declined, it happened quickly. I rode with her in the ambulance on her last ride to the hospital, with Erich following in his pickup truck. As soon as Mom had been diagnosed, Erich had quit whatever job he had at the time, driven from Connecticut to Arizona, and moved in to help take care of her. For all of his defiance as a child, Erich turned out to have the softest heart of all of us—and, as an adult, the deepest sense of connection to our parents. Mom could see him through the back window of the ambulance, and that put her at ease. She waved at him from the gurney, then smiled and said, "I've had so many adventures."

Eleven

AFTER MY MOTHER DIED, I began to feel antsy. Raising a child is a creative act, yes, and being a parent is a role no one should disdain, but it's a role that leaves you feeling both full and empty at the same time. All your instincts tell you that you ought to be gaining a sense of control as time passes, but in fact, you are steadily losing it. It's like operating an avatar, only the avatar has a mind of its own and gets better every day at overriding your commands. Parenting books tell you that this is how it's supposed to work, but the adjustment is stressful.

This is when you start to feel like you wouldn't mind returning to work or taking up a hobby or joining a book club. You want to do something that is all your own, something that your avatar can't fiddle with.

And you want little opportunities to *let loose*. I'm not talking about putting a lampshade on your head. I mean having an uninterrupted conversation with your spouse or watching a whole movie all the way through or writing for a whole morning. When you're raising a child, you're always having to keep one foot on the brake. Actually, you *are* the brake. Some people seem to think that a parent's most important job is to love his or her child. That's not really a parent's job, any more than it is a wife's job to love her husband or vice versa. You can't roll up your sleeves and decide to love your child, but you can roll up your sleeves and decide to chop those green beans a little smaller so that Sweet Pea will stop throwing them across the room and start putting them in her mouth. Your *job* is to prevent unnecessary mishaps, deprivations, and hardships. Don't do this, don't do that, watch out for this, what on earth were you thinking, be careful for god's sake, hold my hand, let go of my leg, slow down, hurry up, and yes, you do need to get these shots, hold still. It's like being in stop-and-go traffic on a freeway that's under permanent construction—sometimes you just want to sneak into the emergency lane, stomp on the gas pedal, and hold it there until your tank runs dry. The day I found myself coming home from Costco with a twelve-pack of spiral notebooks stashed under the mountain of Huggies, I knew it was time to start writing again.

But not yet. We still had to move. We ended up buying a fixer that spring, a house that hadn't been lived in for years. A water pipe had burst inside it, windows were broken, and the yard was a dirt nightmare with a cage for a guard dog rusting near the entrance. I'm not going to describe what the "fixing" process was like, except to say that it kept me too busy to write. When the last permit had been pulled, the last concrete pad had been poured, the last frame built, the last appliance delivered, the last toilet replaced, the last countertop fitted, and the last sheet of insulation unrolled—and after I'd moved all our belongings myself with a rental truck—then, at last, I started writing.

With deeply mixed feelings, we hired someone to help watch Ava for a few hours a day. One day, when I was on my way out the door to go to the library, Ava grabbed my leg and pleaded with me not to go. "I don't want to ever let you go away!" she wailed. I carried her into her room and read with her on my lap until she calmed down, and then she said, "It's OK, you can go now." I put her in her crib with her fluffy blanket and stepped out of her room, but I gave in to a foolish impulse to linger outside her door for a few moments to make sure she was OK. I couldn't help myself; I even peeked back into her room. She was staring up at the sky through her window, and this is what I overhead her say aloud to herself: "You said you'd always be there for me. But you're not."

It's from *The Lion King*; it's what Simba says when he realizes that his dead father isn't looking out for him from his place among the stars after all. Children say the darndest things. I wanted to throw myself into the path of a train.

I gave up on the idea of writing at the library and turned the bedroom next to Ava's into my office. I began work on a novel set in thirteenth-century Asia, about a European captured by the Mongols during the height of their conquest period. Even with childcare help, I could only find time to write three days a week for two hours at a stretch, but that was better than nothing. One unexpected result of being so busy, faced with so many tasks that weren't complicated at all but required my immediate and undivided attention, was that when I did sit down to write, I got to work right away. I didn't waste any time procrastinating. I began to think that maybe, if I didn't procrastinate at all, I could end up writing just as much as I did before having kids. Maybe I wouldn't have to give up anything at all, the way my mother and so many of her friends had. I knew it was possible to write novels and host playdates at the same time, because I'd read in *People* magazine that J. K. Rowling had done it. Not only did she write the first Harry Potter book while she was a stay-at-home parent, she was a *single mom* when she did it. If she could write a book like that without the help of either a spouse or a babysitter, then I, with my terrific support team, had no excuse. I told my editor I would have the Mongol novel finished in two years.

J. K. Rowling is a statistical anomaly. Either that or she is not a real person at all. I think she's a literary hoax, the invention of a group of English professors at Cambridge who played *Dungeons & Dragons* together for thirty years and finally said, "Let's write a book that every kid on earth will want to read!" "Brilliant! And let's say it was written by a single mom; then parents will buy it too!"

My deadline came and went. Life had other plans for the author of *Harry Potter and the Mongol Hordes*.

"Ava needs a sibling," Jessica said to me one day, and I knew better than to argue. Our second daughter was born nine months later, and my domestic duties increased. But I kept writing, and after three years I had a draft of the novel finished. I thought it was brilliant, but alas, no one else did. The main character, both my editor and agent agreed, lacked something. What he lacked, apparently, was character. Lots of things happened to him: He participated in great battles, he watched as cities burned and nations fell, and he even got to have sex, which was new for me. (For some reason, my fictional characters never seem to get laid.) In spite of all that, Catalano del Saggio remained a cipher. Who is this man, and why should we care about him? This was the question that my team put to me, and when I found that my best answer was that he was somebody who wanted to get back to Europe, I knew that I had to start over again.

I decided that while the first draft had plenty of man vs. nature conflict in it, and even more of the man vs. man variety, what it lacked was a good dose of man vs. himself, which just happens to be the kind of conflict I know the most about. Catalano del Saggio needed to feel that something within him was either missing or broken. His sufferings as a captive of the Mongols, I decided, would force him to look inward and resolve this problem. I found an upstairs storage room at Ava's preschool, where I set myself up with a chair and a computer table and worked every morning while either Jessica or our sitter watched baby Esme. Earplugs kept the lyrics of "The Itsy Bitsy Spider" and "I'm a Little Teapot" from distracting me.

For this draft, I made Catalano del Saggio a young Franciscan monk who is captured by the Mongols in 1241 as they storm through present-day Bosnia. After a grueling forced march across

Eurasia, he is assigned the task of translating the Bible for his masters. (Nestorian Christianity was a popular religion among members of Genghis Khan's family, but no translation of the Bible existed in the Mongol language at that time.) Del Saggio's faith in an omnipotent, loving God is strong, but the horrors he witnesses as he travels with the Mongol army plant the seeds of doubt in his mind. He is tested further when he falls in love with a fellow prisoner, a Chinese woman forced to become the concubine of a Mongol prince. When the evil prince is banished by a rival within the Mongol royal family, del Saggio breaks his vow of celibacy to live with the Chinese woman and help her care for her infant son. In the end, the Mongols accuse del Saggio of treason, bind him to a crucifix on the plains of Dzungaria, and leave him for dead. His suffering causes him to lose hope; his faith in a personal God vanishes like a mirage. When all seems lost, he has a spiritual awakening and finds inner peace. Then the Mongols change their minds and cut him down.

I was a little concerned when I printed this draft and it turned out to be only one hundred pages long. I widened the margins and used a bigger font and managed to get the number of pages up to 130, but to no avail—my support network gave it the thumbs-down again. The characters were insufficiently developed, they said. The novel read like an outline that went on too long rather than a story that ended too quickly.

At that point, I'd already spent four years trying to develop Catalano del Saggio's character, and I couldn't think of anything else to do with him. Make him a French Crusader? An English traitor? A medieval bodybuilder? In the meantime, Ava was finishing second grade and baby Esme was preparing to enter kindergarten. Perhaps, I began to think, the problem with my novel couldn't be solved by tinkering with the details. Medieval Europe had never captured my imagination, whereas medieval Asia certainly had. Why, I wondered, had I chosen to stick an Italian into a story that was so clearly Chinese, both geographically and philosophically?

I ended up where I probably should have begun: in Lin'an, the capital of Song dynasty China, on the eve of the Mongol invasion in 1276. For my third draft, I chose for a main character Yin Lu, a young Confucian scholar whose father was one of the most prominent officials serving in the imperial court. Yin Lu wants to live up to his father's example of attempting to restore harmony to the world through the practice of virtue, self-discipline, and enlightened scholarship, but three obstacles stand in his way: (1) He stutters, which makes him seem indecisive; (2) He falls in love with an inappropriate woman; and (3) The Mongols have declared war on China and threatened to turn the whole country into a wasteland if the Song emperor won't surrender.

Here was a story I could sink my teeth into: how the experience of war turned a troubled idealist into a contented fatalist—a Confucian into a Taoist, in other words. I wrote it in a year, sent the manuscript in, and waited for the congratulatory call from New York. I got a discouraging letter instead. That's when my rabbit-whiskers began to tremble.

And that's when Jessica looked at me from across the dinner table one night, with the girls sitting on either side of her, and said, "We need a dog."

Twelve

I'M NOT TERRIBLY ENTHUSIASTIC ABOUT pets but my wife is. In 1989, the year that we were married, Jessica said she wanted to buy a saltwater fish tank. By then, I'd already agreed to two cats (Fog and Smog, the ones I kept off my lap with the tinfoil skirt), so I figured, *Fine, bring on the fish, maybe the smell of the ocean will cancel out the smell of the kitty litter.* "But it's your tank," I said to her. "You have to clean it."

She got a fifty-gallon tank—it was about four feet across and two feet high—and stocked it with a few anemones and a pair of clownfish. This was before *Finding Nemo* came out, so I'd never seen a clownfish before she brought these two home. An interesting fact about clownfish, which was not mentioned in *Finding Nemo,* is that they are transsexuals. They are all born male, and then the largest and most dominant member of the colony becomes female. When she dies, the next male in line swaps gender and takes her place. One of our clowns was a bit larger than the other, so I assumed he was a she.

They are beautiful creatures, I'll admit that, but for me, there's not much else you can do with a fish but stare at it. The novelty wore off after a few months. Meanwhile, the Plexiglas walls became clouded with mineral deposits. Jessica did clean the tank following the terms of our agreement, but not as often as the guy at the pet store had recommended. The anemones eventually gave way to a forest of invasive green algae, and the gravel teemed with brightly colored microscopic organisms. A plaque at the base of our aquarium identifying the featured animals might have read, "Clownfish, Snails, Scum."

Jessica fed them live bloodworms every other day. Live bloodworms, which must be stored in the refrigerator, produce an astonishing volume of waste matter that fouls the water of whatever container you hold them in and smells awful. And a lot of them die before they reach the fish tank, adding to the odor problem. Whenever we left home to travel, we had to arrange for someone to come to the house every other day to feed the worms to the fish and add water to the tank. When we'd had the clownfish for ten years, I asked Jessica if we could give them away and retire the tank, but she wouldn't hear of it. When Jessica gets a pet, she never gives up on it. Ever.

The first of the clownfish—the male, I think—passed away after we'd had him for nineteen years. I assumed that Jessica would want to buy another one to keep the survivor company, but to my surprise she announced that when the second clownfish died, we could drain the tank and move it into the garage. We had children by then—we didn't need fish anymore.

A year later, we found the second transsexual floating upside down in the algae, and it was all I could do to keep from pumping my fist in the air and shouting "Huzzah!" But four days later, the aquarium lights were still on and the filters were still running. Was Jessica observing a mourning period? Or had she changed her mind about retiring the tank? As casually as I could, I asked her if she needed any help draining the water out of it.

"We can't do that yet," she said.

"Why not?"

"Because there are still snails in it."

For a moment, I thought she was kidding, but then I saw that she wasn't, and I got annoyed. I think it's endearing that Jessica rescues slugs from the sidewalk, and I can handle the fact that she won't let me kill wasps when they drink out of our swimming pool, but this was going too far. I was not going to hire a sitter to feed the snails.

Anticipating my objections, Jessica said, "I'll find someone who wants them when I have time. Right now, I don't have time."

I couldn't argue with the not-having-time part; with my career in a tailspin, she was supporting all four of us by herself. Finding adoptive homes for her snails was the least I could do, so I got proactive. I found a Vietnamese-owned aquarium supply shop that agreed to take them. I fished the trio of snails out of the tank, put them into a container, and made my way to the shop. When I showed them to the proprietor, he frowned. "Where snails?" he asked.

"Right there," I said, but I felt myself blush. Compared to the healthy-looking animals in the tanks around me, my snails looked awful. Their shells were covered with so much algae and sea-hair that you couldn't tell they were snails at all. I reached in and tugged at them to show they were clinging to the bottom of the Tupperware container. Dead snails can't do that, I pointed out. I handed it over, and when he asked if I wanted the container back, I said no. I was afraid that if I said yes, he might hand it to me with the snails still in it.

When I got home it was late afternoon. I made cocktails for Jessica and me and announced that I'd found a home for all three of our snails.

"Three?" she said, looking confused at first and then slightly suspicious. "There were *four* snails in there."

I made a second trip to the aquarium store the next day.

What can we learn from the clownfish/snail incident? Mainly, I think, that my kids got better DNA from their mother than from me. Let's run a comparison:

My wife's circle of empathy is so wide that it includes even snails—an admirable trait; I think of snails as plants with shells.

She gets what she wants—an enviable trait; I wave the white flag and *then* negotiate terms—an inferior strategy.

She earns more than I do—an unsettling trait; I claim that it doesn't bother me at all, but my nose grows and other parts of me shrink every time I say it.

And finally, she has *ballast*. No one needs to tell her what to do with snails or how to vote or the right way to make a film or raise children; she figures these things out on her own without a whole lot of fuss or indecision. Something keeps her on an even keel no matter how rough the seas get, and she has total confidence in her internal navigation system. She has faith to burn, in other words, although if you ask her what she believes in, she'll probably tell you that she doesn't know and doesn't even think about it.

This, if you ask me, is *the* trait that separates those fortunate souls who lead charmed, purpose-driven lives from those of us—like me—who are screwed.

When Jessica said that the girls needed a dog, I breathed deeply and counted to ten before responding. This was one battle that I did not want to lose. As a compromise, I suggested that we invest in a realistic, battery-operated dog puppet. That's how we'd handled the horse question, and it worked beautifully. You'd never know that the pony in Ava's room isn't real, and no one's been talking about stables or riding lessons since. But no, Jessica insisted, it wouldn't do for our kids to have a dog puppet when all their friends have real dogs. And believe me, every family in our neighborhood has a dog. I know this because every one of them barks at me when I take my walk. And there are few sounds on earth I hate more than the sound of a barking dog.

I don't have anything against dogs as animals. Like bears and dolphins and sea snakes, they are perfectly fine creatures. They are children of the universe, as the author of the "Desiderata" might say; they have a right to be here. It's dogs as family pets that get on my nerves. Dogs require a lot of attention, and if they don't get it—and let's face it, most of them don't—they become nuisances. I'm talking about the barkers, the roamers, the garbage can tippers, the carpet soakers, the sidewalk crappers, the car chasers, the jumpers, the diggers, the droolers, the crotch-seeking missiles. I'm talking about the Average American Suburban Family Dog—the AASFaD, for short.

Jessica feels differently about AASFaDs than I do. She, her parents, and her two siblings have owned so many of these creatures between them that I've lost count. As far as I can tell, they're all the same dog only with different-size ears. This dog-of-many-ears isn't mean or dangerous, and it is certainly loyal to the humans who feed it. My complaint is that this composite dog—and its composite owner, whom I adore and admire in every other way—cannot imagine that anything a nonbiting dog does could possibly get on a person's nerves. And if anything short of biting does get on someone's nerves, it's the person's fault. The person must be uptight and unable to recognize a "happy" dog when they see it. A happy dog, by my relatives' definition, is one that does pretty much whatever it wants and receives unconditional love from human beings, and unconditional love is what all dogs receive from my in-laws, bless their hearts. And I do mean all dogs. Lucky indeed is the mud-soaked, half-starved, three-legged, blind, diabetic stray who wanders within sight of a Yu, because that dog will be a stray no longer. It will henceforth be a dog with a name and a home, and it will be happy—but it will not receive much in the way of training. He's happy and that's all that matters. If he doesn't feel like sitting or staying, or if he doesn't feel like resisting the impulse to bark, well, he's just a dog being a dog. What's the big deal?

On this point, I thought Jessica and I had come to an agreement: no dogs. She's an insomniac who rarely gets more than four hours of sleep at night, and those four hours usually fall between four and eight in the morning—unless a dog wakes her up. Which is what happens when we go up north to visit her parents. Destry, their golden retriever, starts barking just before dawn, but it's not his fault. He's just responding to the commotion in the front yard, where John and Connie's roosters compete with their peacocks and geese for the title of Loudest Domestic Fowl.

Allow me to present this English-language transcript of the opera that is performed there at first light every morning:

ROOSTER: LISTEN TO THIS! DO YOU BELIEVE THIS? YOU CAN'T *TOUCH* THIS!
DOG: HEY! HEY! *HEY!! HEY HEY HEY HEY!!!!*
CHICKENS: Dog bad. Dog bad.
DUCKS: We live in mud. We stand in our own poop. Life is like that.
GEESE: MAKE WAY, FUCKERS!
SEXUALLY FRUSTRATED MALE PEACOCK: PLEEEEEEE-ASE! Let it be TODAAAAAY!
INDIFFERENT FEMALE PEACOCK: With a tail like that? *THINK AGAIN.*
ROOSTER: AMATEURS, ALL OF YOU! AMATEURS!
DOG: HEY! HEY! *HEY!!!*
CHICKS: help help help help help help . . .

My in-laws don't just love dogs; they love all animals. They've built an honest-to-goodness, Vermont-style barn in their front yard just to hold the food for them. Jessica grew up surrounded by pets and can't imagine life without them. I've done my best to accommodate her wishes—I thought I'd been a pretty good sport about the fish and snails and the zebra finches and the cockatiel and the Chinese robin and the two cats and the guinea pigs—but I drew the line at dogs. No, I said. This is nonnegotiable. We are not getting a dog.

Imagine that! A rabbit telling an eagle how to feather her nest!

Nothing obstructs Jessica's will, because she has never met a problem she couldn't solve. She researches, she considers, she decides, and then she tells me what we've decided to do. In this case, we decided to adopt a pretrained adult dog that had been rescued from a shelter.

Jessica went online and found an outfit in North Carolina that caters to clients who don't have the time to housebreak or train a puppy. The husband and wife who own this company rescue abandoned dogs and then train them before finding adoptive homes for them. Our dog, Jessica assured me, would not chew, it would not dig, it would not jump, it would not chase, it would not sniff human asses or lunge at human crotches. We would give this wonder hound a home, and in return it would play dead all day and night, and everyone would be happy.

"You're going to love having a dog," Jessica assured me. "It's so obvious."

That's exactly what she'd said about having children, and as she will happily tell you given only the slightest encouragement, she was right—about having kids, that is. In theory, the same thing would happen to me once we got a dog. I would fall in love with it and wonder why I'd waited so long to come around.

I dreaded the arrival of the AASFaD, but since it took several months for a dog to be selected and trained, I thought less and less about it, until I'd managed to forget about it completely. I had bigger problems to think about that spring: The economy had collapsed, we had two kids, our savings had nearly run out, and I owed my publisher a novel. They had paid me an advance for it six years earlier, and I had written the book three different ways, but none of them had been accepted. What was I going to do?

Remember my epiphany about the relationship between creativity and conscious will? The one that made me feel so free? Well, now it worked against me. Believing that I couldn't force the Muse meant that, for all I knew, I might spend another six years writing another book that turned out to be a dud. Book sales were down across the board, bookstores were going out of business, and every week there was some new story in the trades about the emergency measures publishers were taking to recoup their losses. I had to start something else, finish it soon, and hope that it turned out to be a story that an editor could love. And this time, I couldn't afford to fail.

Thirteen

IN MARCH OF 2009, I woke up in the middle of the night feeling that something was not right with my breathing. The rhythm was normal, but I felt as though not enough oxygen was getting into my blood. The air in the room felt thin. I yawned a few times and opened the window next to my bed, but the feeling remained. What happened next wasn't subtle. A shock wave of adrenaline propelled me out of bed. It was as if I were reacting to a gunshot that my body had felt but my ears had not heard. A tingling sensation burst out from the center of my chest and then ran down into my limbs and up into my head. My heart rate shot up to nearly three times its resting pace, and I was having lots of skipped beats, and then my left arm and the left side of my chest began to feel tight.

I thought: *I'm forty-nine years old, I've got two young daughters, and I'm having a heart attack. Shit!*

In order to get her four hours of sleep, Jessica creates her own Fortress of Solitude each night out of cloth, memory foam, and Ambien. She forms a boundary around herself with a U-shaped body pillow, lays a folded towel over her eyes, inserts soft earplugs, and then covers her head with a second pillow. I couldn't bring myself to wake her up (I wasn't thinking very clearly, obviously), so I stumbled out to the kitchen. But then I realized that if I collapsed there, the kids would find me when they got up wanting breakfast.

That's when the terror set in. I'm a guy who knows what anxiety feels like, and this was not anxiety. I'd never felt anything like it. In the first *Star Wars* movie, there is a scene where a spaceship makes the "leap to hyperspace," meaning it attains the speed of light. The characters in the ship are looking out the window at the stars when it happens. The stars begin as fixed points in empty space, but when the leap occurs, the stars stretch out into lines, and then—*pow!*—the ship is gone. That's what the leap from anxiety to terror feels like. One moment I was aware of clear, distinct thoughts in my mind, then they suddenly got stretched until they were unrecognizable, and then—*whoosh!*—the part of me that feels like "me" was gone. Instead, there was just animal fear.

I put a cordless phone in my hand, but I couldn't remember the sequence of numbers that you dial when you need help. I stood there, frozen, too scared to do anything. I tried sitting down and breathing deeply, but the moment I sat down, another explosion of adrenaline propelled me out of the chair. If you have ever stepped off the curb of a street only to have a car or bus roar past you, inches away, with its horn blaring, you will recognize the subsequent experience: a sense of tingling heat rushing throughout your body and then a wave of trembling, sickening weakness. I paced in the kitchen until my heart rate went down and my thoughts began to clear; then I put on my clothes and walked very gingerly up and down the driveway, still with the cordless phone in my hand, until dawn. Ava and Esme came down for breakfast at around six o'clock, and feeding them and getting them ready for school kept me focused and made me feel slightly better. Still, when our housekeeper, Olga, arrived at seven thirty, she looked aghast when she saw me.

"Your face is green," she said.

I told her that I didn't feel well and asked her to take over. I roused Jessica from the Fortress of Solitude and told her that I had to see a doctor, but I assured her that I would be fine to drive myself to the hospital. Halfway there, I had another spell of whatever was going on. This time, I felt as if my consciousness were somehow being pressed from all sides, and crushed down to a small point, and that if it got any smaller, I would pass out. Individual words appeared in my mind, words like "car" and "phone" and "hospital," but they didn't line up in any sort of coherent pattern. I pressed as hard as I could against the floor of the car with my left foot, thinking somehow that the muscular effort would keep me from passing out, and I kept driving.

Checking in took only a few moments. The nurse led me to a room, told me to lie down and remove my shirt, and got me hooked up to a machine right away. The results of this test indicated that I was not having a heart attack, at least not at that moment. The doctor on call looked me over and listened to my chest with his stethoscope, noted the palpitations, and detected a heart murmur. He paged a cardiologist.

Meanwhile, my heart rate had gone down to eighty beats per minute, and the other symptoms had diminished. While we waited for the cardiologist to arrive, the doctor asked if I drank heavily, if I used any recreational drugs, if I smoked, if I was taking any medications, and so on. When I answered no to all of those questions, he asked about my diet, exercise, and sleep habits. I described what I ate and told him that I exercised nearly every day, slept well, meditated regularly, and had been doing tai chi for thirty years.

Been under any unusual stress lately, he asked? Financial problems? Marital strain? Depression?

I told him that I was a writer who was having a hard time finishing a book, and soon I was going to have to share my house with a dog, but other than that, I had plenty to be thankful for. I'd been happily married for twenty years, had two beautiful children, and my wife was working steadily. No lawsuits, no foreclosure notices, no crazy neighbors.

The cardiologist arrived and, after listening to my heart for a while with a stethoscope and doing a lot of frowning, recommended that I visit his office later that morning for more extensive tests. An hour later, I watched in awe as he passed what looked like a computer mouse over my chest, generating a full-color, real-time, moving image of the inside of my heart onto a screen right next to me. The cardiologist determined that my valves were working properly and that the murmur was benign. He advised me to contact him if the symptoms came back but otherwise not to worry. As we get older, he said, things happen.

I went home feeling giddy in the way that only someone who believes he has just dodged a bullet can feel. I picked up the girls from school, and they never looked more beautiful than they did that afternoon. The four of us went out for dinner, and then we sat on the couch in the living room under blankets and took turns reading stories aloud. I went to bed that night feeling grateful for everything and fell asleep at my usual hour. Then, at two o'clock, another explosion of adrenaline woke me from a deep sleep. My body lurched out of bed again, and I did exactly as I had done the night before, putting the cordless phone into my hand and pacing until the symptoms died down.

I felt discouraged in the way that only someone who thinks he has dodged a bullet, only to see the bullet change course in midair and head right back toward him, can feel. The spells kept coming every hour or so until dawn. At seven o'clock, I called the cardiologist's office, and the receptionist told me to be there by eight but not to hesitate to dial 911 if I felt it was an emergency. Was it an emergency? I felt, in a classic example of irrational, magical thinking, that if I made the dreaded emergency call and summoned an ambulance to my home, I would somehow tip the scales of reality in favor of catastrophe. By refusing to make that call, I was holding tragedy at bay through sheer force of will. Still, I glanced at my image in the bathroom mirror and saw that Olga had not been exaggerating—my face was, in fact, green.

I made it to the cardiologist's office, but by the time I got there the symptoms had died down again. He attached me to a portable, twenty-four-hour heart monitor and told me to wear it under my clothes until the following day and then to bring it in so the information could be downloaded and examined. He advised me not to change anything about my daily routine—not to make any effort to be unusually calm or relaxed.

That night, I was supposed to take Ava to a special event at the Museum of Natural History. She had been looking forward to this event for months. Ava was obsessed with paleontology and all matters dinosaurian that year, so although I was feeling shaky from my experiences the previous two nights and concerned that I might have another spell during the dinner event, I decided that I couldn't bear to make Ava miss this opportunity. With sensors plastered to my chest, wires running under my shirt, and the heart monitor hidden in my pants pocket, we drove downtown, and the event was all that it had been cracked up to be and more. Before dinner, we received a tour of the museum's new Tyrannosaurus Rex exhibit, and Ava had the chance to ask the paleontologists questions while they cleaned and prepared an actual T. Rex skeleton. Ava and I were both enthralled, and I had no unpleasant symptoms all evening. Once again, I went to bed that night feeling very happy to be alive and confident that all would be well. I didn't wake up at all that night and felt fine the next morning. I turned in the machine at noon, and later that afternoon, the cardiologist called to say that everything looked normal. He scheduled me for a treadmill stress test the following week and advised me, as before, to be concerned but not fearful and to take a "wait and see" attitude.

The next day, once the kids had been dropped off at school and preschool, I decided to try getting some writing done. I sat down at my desk and looked over what I had written a few days earlier but found it nearly impossible to concentrate. By the time I read to the end of a sentence, I had lost track of how the sentence had begun. Writing was out of the question; I couldn't hold even the simplest thought in mind long enough to connect it to other thoughts.

Understandably, the discovery that I couldn't think straight made me feel anxious. To calm myself, I tried closing my eyes and counting my breaths. I got to the number five and then—*bang!* Another spell struck. This was the first time it had happened during the day.

Something about daylight makes unpleasant experiences more bearable than having them in darkness. I felt less terrified by what was going on this time, and besides, this had happened several times already and I had not dropped dead, and I'd been seen by a doctor and a cardiologist twice, so it seemed likely that I would survive this episode. Something was wrong with me—that was certain—but I felt pretty confident that it wasn't going to kill me that day. I left the house and went for a walk. When the symptoms had passed, I decided to try doing my tai chi routine to see how that felt. It felt good at first, but just as I felt my mind beginning to relax—*bang!* Another spell.

Walking briskly seemed to be the most effective response to the symptoms. Knowing that I had a scheduled appointment with the cardiologist the following week, I decided against any more trips to the hospital unless something radically different happened. I had another spell that evening, just as I was falling asleep, and then two more in the hours between three and five o'clock in the morning.

A few hours later that morning, while I sat in the house not really knowing what to do with myself, a dear friend of mine—a neurosurgeon, no less—called to say that the operation he was supposed to perform that morning had been cancelled. Would I like to meet him for lunch? he asked. "Would I ever!" I said. An hour later, we met at Descanso Gardens, a beautiful spot with a small café set up near the entrance, and I think that poor Srinath was a little taken aback by how glad I appeared to be to see him. I barely gave him any chance to eat as I described what was going on.

It must be hard for doctors to have to hear their friends' medical crisis stories, but he responded with just the right combination of sympathy and clinical detachment. He said that a heart-valve disorder would have been his first guess as to the origin of my symptoms, but since that had already been ruled out, he leaned toward anxiety as the most likely culprit. Then he told me that he himself, after suffering from a bout of stress-related depression, had been treated with a form of hypnosis therapy. He found it so helpful that he decided to learn the technique himself so that he could use it to treat those among his patients who would likely benefit from relaxation exercises. He invited me to come over to his house that night and we would give it a try.

This lifted my spirits. After dinner, I drove to his place, and after his wife had put their two kids to bed, Srinath had me settle into a reclining chair. He put a pillow behind my head and covered me up to the neck in a blanket, and then he led me through a visualization exercise that was deeply relaxing. But at the most relaxing point of all, just when I felt as clear as water and as light as air, the adrenaline burst in my chest again and my heart started racing again.

How disappointed I felt! It seemed to me that if the source of the problem were anxiety rather than an organic pathology, it wouldn't make sense for me to have the attacks when I was most relaxed. Srinath told me not to be discouraged, however, and advised me to try going through the exercise on my own once or twice a day for the next week. I promised to let him know how it was going, and then I went home, where I spent another night without getting much sleep.

The spells kept coming, every few hours, all through that

weekend and the following week. I saw the cardiologist again, took the treadmill test, and passed it. He said that he'd done pretty much all that he could do and suggested that I see an internist. I scheduled an appointment with one for the following week and just held on as the spells came more and more frequently, although in no discernible pattern. Some woke me from a deep sleep, others came when I was sitting at my desk, others when I was reading aloud to my daughters, others when I was outdoors walking. They came most consistently, however, whenever I made any sort of conscious effort to relax my mind, so I stopped trying to do that.

When the spells occurred, I couldn't think at all. It was as if a blizzard were taking place in my head: whiteout conditions, zero visibility. I could carry out mechanical tasks, like cooking or driving or washing the dishes, but I couldn't hold a conversation or dial a telephone number. My short-term memory was completely wiped out; anything that required holding sequences of words or numbers in mind became impossible. By the twelfth day of this ordeal, I felt exhausted and discouraged. It was all I could do just to get through each day, one hour at a time, sometimes one minute at a time, and the symptoms were changing. Now I was experiencing chills, fits of violent trembling, and hot flashes. On the morning of the thirteenth day, the attacks were occurring every five to seven minutes, and the feeling of confusion and discomfort got so intense that I called Srinath in desperation and asked what I should do. "Get to a hospital right away," he said, and so once again, I drove myself to the emergency room, checked in, and then sat in the waiting room for two hours while a team of construction workers wielding jackhammers tore up the floor a few yards away. Just my luck—I was having the most frightening experience of my life during our hospital's remodeling project.

The sense of being crushed from all sides, of hanging on to consciousness by my fingernails, and of indescribable, imminent danger became overwhelming. I gripped the arms of the chair in the waiting room as tightly as I could, feeling that this was somehow all that was keeping me from blacking out. Convinced that I was about to lose either my mind or my life at any moment, I begged the triage nurse for a pen and a piece of paper and scrawled a farewell message to my wife and daughters. When, at last, my turn to be seen came, a new ER doctor looked me over, and after hearing the results of all my tests from the last two weeks, he said, "You're having panic attacks. Very common these days, what with the recession and all."

"There must be some mistake," I said. I explained that I wasn't afraid of elevators or bridges or public speaking and that the spells were arriving unexpectedly, regardless of what I was doing or thinking about. They even happened when I was meditating. How can a person have a panic attack when he's meditating?

The doctor all but rolled his eyes. He wrote me a prescription for fifteen tablets of a tranquilizer and told me to "follow up," meaning consult a shrink. I went to the pharmacy, bought the pills, and took one. Fifteen minutes later, my symptoms were gone. For the first time in nearly two weeks, I felt as if I could think clearly.

I drove straight from the hospital to my local bookstore, bought the most scientific-looking book on panic disorders I could find, and then went home and read it. To my dismay, the book described my symptoms—and my perfectionist, self-flagellating personality—with eerie precision. To my relief, I learned that panic attacks are quite common, not "organ-threatening," and highly treatable. While they can indeed be triggered by specific circumstances, such as having to drive over a bridge or get in an elevator or give a speech, they can also strike unexpectedly. You would think that learning to relax would be the key to overcoming the disorder, but for some of us, it isn't that simple. *Deliberate* attempts to relax—by meditating, for example—can actually trigger the attacks or make the symptoms worse.

For us, the way to manage the attacks is counterintuitive. If trying to relax doesn't work, then we have to stop trying. A crucial step toward gaining control over the disorder is to become less afraid of the symptoms. The more willing we are to surrender to them, the more quickly they pass.

Armed with this knowledge and my fourteen remaining tablets of lorazepam, I set out to cure myself of this affliction. Each time I felt the surge of adrenaline and the avalanche of unpleasant symptoms, I imagined I was a scientist conducting an experiment, and my only duty was to experience what happened and record the data. The experiences, I reassured myself, would be transient and of no lasting significance. Within a week of approaching the attacks in this way, I was down to only two or three a day, and after each spell, I was able to recover my sense of mental stability and clarity within minutes rather than hours. By the end of the second week, the crisis had passed; the attacks had been downgraded from hurricane status to mild showers. I felt shaky but stable.

It may seem puzzling that someone who would go right out and buy a book about panic attacks written by a psychiatrist, and then follow its advice, wouldn't simply make an appointment to *see* a psychiatrist. If the help is out there, why not make use of it? I live in Los Angeles, the therapy capital of the world—you can't throw a rock in this town without hitting a Jungian or a Reichian or a transactional analyst—yet I never considered heeding the ER doctor's advice that I "follow up." I think this requires some explanation.

I come with baggage. Part of it is temperamental: The kind of guy who can't bring himself to wake up his wife when he thinks he's having a heart attack and insists on driving himself to the hospital doesn't feel comfortable asking for help. Another reason is that I was raised by a social worker—a professional counselor—who, over the course of his forty-year career, became deeply disillusioned with psychotherapy. "Breakthrough" theories and pop psychology fads came and went, along with their television-ready celebrity proponents, but the suffering continued. In the long run, he concluded, the people he knew who underwent therapy, himself included, didn't seem to get any better than the ones who declined treatment or couldn't afford it.

Whether my father's assessment was accurate or not, it is surely true that therapy only works if you trust your therapist. Having inherited my father's skepticism, I have always felt the same resistance toward the idea of lying down on a therapist's couch as I feel toward the thought of sitting down in a priest's confessional. If the faith isn't there, what's the point?

And finally, there is the fact that I am a writer. I don't, under any circumstances, want to be told how my central conflicts ought to be resolved, whether fictional or real. I feel compelled to work them out on my own. The solution to the problems that define me *must* come from within rather than outside of me, otherwise the dissonance goes unresolved. Being a competent writer doesn't make me a competent therapist, of course—but for better or worse, I am the only therapist I know how to trust. That's my baggage.

I made it through the month of April without any panic attacks, but I was still feeling shaky. One day I had to take Esme to the pediatrician's office for a couple of vaccinations, and on the way she started crying.

"I'm afraid!" she wailed. "Can you give me a grown-up pill so I won't cry?"

I wanted to say, "You and me both, honey."

I felt like a wounded animal that just wanted to curl up in a den and stay still for a while, but we ended up having a busy month instead. During Ava's spring break from school, the four of us took a little trip north to visit Jessica's parents. From there, we drove to Sonoma County to spend a few nights at a place called Safari West, where you sleep in semipermanent tents on the grounds of the park while exotic birds whoop and cheetahs bark and giraffes saunter by only a few yards away. On our first night there, Esme lost her first tooth, so we decided to have dinner at a nice restaurant in town to celebrate. Jessica was the second child in her family, and like a lot of later-borns, she wants to make sure that the younger sibling's childhood accomplishments get equal attention, so she does her best to make sure that little Esme gets her due. During this dinner, while showing her tooth for the umpteenth time to Ava, Esme lost her grip on it. It somehow fell into a crack between her upholstered, bench-style seat and the wall, and she started to cry. If this had happened in an Applebee's, I probably wouldn't have minded, but this was a boutique restaurant with only a dozen tables in it, so the sound of her crying seemed especially out of place. The waiter came by and valiantly offered to use a screwdriver to remove the back of the seat from the wall so that he could retrieve the tooth. As he went to fetch the screwdriver, Ava, who was distressed to see how upset Esme was, suddenly leapt from her seat to help look for the tooth, lost her balance, and fell across our table. The table had been cleared for dessert but still had two glasses filled with red wine on it, along with the half-empty wine bottle. The table lurched so violently that the two glasses and the bottle launched into the air, sent their contents flying in all directions, and then landed on the floor in an inverted rainbow of Merlot and broken glass. My anxiety level shot so high that I knew I could not survive another moment in that room without starting to panic. I took the two girls by the hand and led them as gently and steadily as I could out the door and to the car while Jessica helped the waiter clean up. When she came out, she said she'd given him a hundred-dollar tip.

By the time we got home, I was exhausted after a full week of travel with two small children. Just getting through airports with kids and their equipment in this post-9/11 world requires patience, and that spring, I had no patience left.

And we had a dog coming. The outfit in North Carolina sent word that our pet was nearly ready for delivery. Another two or three weeks at the most. Jessica and the girls were ecstatic, but every morning when I took my walk and the neighborhood gargoyles assaulted me with their infernal barking, I felt like a prison guard walking the tier and thought: *In a few weeks, one of these things is going to be living in my house. What if I can't handle the barking?*

I tried to imagine explaining to the girls that we would have to find another home for their dog because it made Daddy nervous. I pictured the awful scene: locking the bewildered animal in its travel crate while my daughters sobbed and my wife cursed me under her breath. I would be the goat, and it would be my fault for letting it go this far.

This family adventure, I thought, *is not going to end well. We've bitten off more than I can chew.*

Fourteen

ON MAY 5, MY BROTHER, Erich, called before dawn. "I don't want to scare you," he said, but when he told me that Rachel was in the intensive care unit of a hospital in Connecticut with severe pneumonia, I got scared. "If there's any way in the world you can get out here," he said, "now would be the time."

I woke Jessica and told her what was going on, and all she said was, "You have to go there right now." She emerged from the bedroom five minutes later with her laptop in her hands. She had booked a seat on a plane to New York for me already and was just confirming the reservation on a rental car.

I made breakfast for Ava and Esme, dropped them off at school, and drove straight from there to the airport. I didn't think I would have enough time to check in any luggage, so I brought only what I could pack in a carry-on suitcase. Good thing, too, because the flight attendants were about to shut the door to the plane when I made it to the gate.

I called Erich just before we took off. He said that Rachel's fever had gone down and she was able to speak again, but for some reason, the infection in her lungs was not responding to antibiotics. He explained to me that just four days earlier, he had invited Rachel and her family over for dinner. Before they started eating,

Rachel said she felt tired and wanted to lie down. She stayed on the couch the whole evening. The next day, she had a fever of 105 and said she felt like she'd been run over by a truck. She was so weak that our father, who was at that time living in a small apartment over Rachel's garage, had to drive her to the doctor's office. The doctor examined her, detected fluid in both of her lungs, and recommended that she check herself in to the hospital right away. Once there, she was sent straight to the ICU, where she began receiving antibiotics, the standard treatment for pneumonia.

She responded well, and after two days was able to move into a regular room. But that night, the infection suddenly got worse. Rachel was moved back to the ICU, and that was when Erich had called me. The doctors, he said, were beginning to suspect that Rachel had contracted an exotic virus on a recent trip she had taken to Costa Rica and Panama.

On the flight east, I decided that I would offer to stay in Rachel's house and help take care of her daughters, Isabela and Livia, until the crisis had passed. The girls were nine and six years old that year—exactly one year older than Ava and Esme. With me watching the girls, Rachel's husband, Daniel, could spend as much time as he needed at the hospital. And who could be better qualified for the job than me? I could take over without missing a beat. As bad as the situation was, I drew some satisfaction from the thought that I could do something for my sister that not all brothers could do.

I arrived late at night. My nieces had already gone to bed, and my father was in the living room waiting for me. He told me that Rachel's condition was about the same and that Daniel was at the hospital with her. My father, whose seventy-ninth birthday was only a few weeks away, looked exhausted. He excused himself and headed back to his apartment for some sleep, and I went upstairs to check on the girls. I looked in their bedroom but saw that both of their beds were empty. Then I remembered that my sister and her husband practiced the "family bed" custom—the children had their own beds but rarely used them. They usually slept with their parents, all four in one bed.

I went back downstairs and began poking through Rachel's shelves for a book to read. It occurred to me, after glancing at a few dozen titles, that I was learning more about my sister by examining her library than I had in the thirty-two years since I had left home for college.

Her interests, as reflected in her choice of reading material, turned out to be nearly identical to my own: psychology, philosophy, and cookbooks for busy parents. I pulled a yellowed paperback off the shelf: *Meditations,* by Marcus Aurelius. A few of the pages had been crimped, which made me curious, so I opened up to the first one and found that she'd marked the following passage:

> For a human soul, the greatest of self-inflicted wrongs is to make itself (so far as it is able to do so) a kind of tumor or abscess on the universe; for to quarrel with circumstances is always a rebellion against Nature—and Nature includes the nature of each individual part.

And on the second marked page, this:

> Let it be clear to you that the peace of green fields can always be yours, in this, that, or any other spot; and that nothing is any different here from what it would be either up in the hills, or down by the sea, or wherever else you will.

Wow, I thought. *My poor sister.* I didn't know that she'd been circling around on the same weary path as me, consulting the Stoics, Alan Watts, Krishnamurti, D. T. Suzuki, and so on. You'd think that I would have enjoyed the sense of a shared interest with her, or of kinship, but I didn't. I just felt sorry.

I didn't get much sleep that first night in Rachel's house, but I got up before anyone else and started poking around the kitchen for breakfast ideas. Daniel's car was parked outside; he must have come home very late. Livia, the younger of the two girls, was the first to make it down the stairs. When she appeared in the kitchen, I stepped forward to give her a hug, but she backed away and stuck out her tongue, and I remembered that she had reacted the exact same way the last time I'd seen her, a year earlier. Rachel had apologized for this and explained to me that Livia wasn't the hugging type.

Isabela came down next, and she *is* the hugging type. Once she had peeled herself off me, she explained that her mommy was in the hospital but would be home soon and then we could all go to the Danbury mall together to the Build-A-Bear store and build bears. While I started fixing breakfast, Isabela played her violin and her recorder for me. Livia asked if she could stir the batter and flip the pancakes and announced that her big sister had memorized an entire Hannah Montana dance routine. "Show him!" Livia commanded, and her older sister ran to fetch a CD player, started the music, and launched into a performance in the kitchen.

Daniel, who is the most hugging type of all, came downstairs while Isabela was dancing, and he nearly crushed me in his embrace. Everything about him is emphatic; his voice can be heard a mile away and his laugh from at least twice that distance. He thanked me profusely for coming and reported that Rachel's condition was stable when he left the hospital at two o'clock and that he was sure the worst was over; she was going to be fine. I offered him a cup of coffee and he took it but apologized for having to run; he had to get to work as soon as possible and finish a job that week or—he told me this quietly so the girls wouldn't overhear it—he and Rachel would not be able to make the mortgage payment on the tile shop building that month.

The recession had been killing them. So even during this crisis, he was still tiling bathrooms all day before rushing over to the hospital to keep Rachel company at night. He poured the coffee into a thermos bottle, grabbed a banana from the counter, and in a roar of tires flying over loose gravel, he and his Tile Shop truck were down the driveway and gone.

I got the girls to stop dancing and eat, fixed their lunches, and made sure they'd put their homework in their backpacks. We walked outside to wait for the bus, and when it came, they boarded it happily and waved to me as it pulled away. I went back inside and called Erich, who was keeping vigil at the hospital. He told me that Rachel was stable for the time being, and he encouraged me to drive over to see her.

Rachel was alert and sitting up in bed when I got to the hospital. She had to wear an oxygen mask but didn't seem to be in any pain. She couldn't talk but she could write on a little pad of paper. She gave me the thumbs-up when I told her that I'd cooked pancakes for the girls for breakfast, and she rolled her eyes when I said that Isabela had performed the Hannah Montana routine for me.

How was Livia? she wrote.

"She helped me cook breakfast," I said, and Rachel looked pleased. I promised her that I'd keep the girls busy and make sure they ate their vegetables, brushed their teeth, washed behind their ears, and observed strict disciplinary protocols. Rachel wrote, *Good luck.*

After our visit, I stepped outside with Erich, and we agreed that she looked pretty good. The doctors were being vague about the condition of her lungs, but she didn't have a fever, and her blood oxygen levels were close to normal. "It's looking better today than it did yesterday," Erich said. "I hope I didn't call you out here for nothing."

A nurse passed by, gave us a smile, and said, "You're sister's looking good today." At that point, I felt inclined to agree with Daniel—the worst seemed over. I called Jessica and told her what I'd seen and heard, and when she asked me how long I thought it would be before Rachel could go home, I guessed another week.

I went back to Rachel's house, cooked lunch for Dad and me,

and decided to do some cleaning. By the time the girls came home from school, I was only half done, so I sent them next door to play with their friends, whose mother, Lisa, said she'd be happy to watch the girls for the afternoon. I got the house straightened up and went out to get some supplies. I came back with a bunch of stuff that I know my girls like to eat, and then I cooked dinner. Daniel came home from work at around six—he looked exhausted—wolfed down some food, and left for the hospital. I read some books aloud to the girls before putting them to bed, but when I tried to turn off the light, Livia howled in protest.

"Livia won't sleep if you don't lie here with us," Isabela explained, so I lay down in the bed between the two of them and stayed there until they had fallen asleep.

Daniel came in at one o'clock. He told me that Rachel had spiked a fever earlier that night, and her oxygen levels had suddenly dropped—either that or her blood pressure, Daniel wasn't exactly sure; it was all so goddamned confusing. Alarms had gone off, and the nurses had had to page a resident to deal with it, but after they'd given Rachel some special drugs, things had calmed down, and the nurses told Daniel to go home and get some sleep.

The next day was Sunday—Mother's Day. Our plan was for Daniel to take the girls over to the hospital to visit Rachel at eleven, when visiting hours started in the ICU, and for them all to have lunch in the room together. The girls had only seen Rachel once since she'd been admitted to the hospital, and that was when she had been in a regular room. I made chocolate chip pancakes for the girls and drove myself over to Erich's place so he and I could take a walk in the hills behind his house. We followed a path that took us up to a high spot in Tarrywile Park, where we sat on a boulder and admired the view. We could even see the hospital from there.

Erich had already visited Rachel that morning, and he said that in spite of her crisis the previous evening, she had slept well. She was still on the ventilator, her heart rate was still up at around 150, and her breathing was shallow and rapid, but the doctors said she was getting stable. He said, "I have a good feeling about today."

Erich showed me some pictures of his son William, who was just six months old, and we shared parental sleep-deprivation stories until it was time to start back down the hill. Erich had made plans to take his wife, Tamiko, their baby, William, and Tamiko's older son, John, out for Mother's Day brunch. I was going to pick up our father from Rachel's house and have lunch with him, then we were all planning to meet at Erich's that evening for a barbecue.

Erich had come a long way since his ill-fated first day at the accounting firm. He'd stuck with that job for a year but never adjusted to it. A series of other accounting-related jobs followed that one, ranging from comptroller at a gravel pit to accounts manager at an equipment rental company. He even managed the books for a nonprofit juvenile boot camp for a while. With each job, he felt challenged at the beginning and hopeful that he'd found his proper vocation rather than just another paycheck, but always, within a year or so, he lost interest. And for him, the feeling of being on a treadmill was unbearable; he had to move on and search elsewhere.

Starting the tile business with Rachel challenged him more than any of his previous jobs had. During their first few years working together, he was having to learn something new almost every day. With number crunching, he could never point to something at the end of the day and say, "I made that," but now he could. Each installation was unique and existed in the physical world. He could look at the kitchens and bathrooms he'd built, admire their appearance, and know that his customers actually used them every day. But after Rachel and Daniel married, Erich began to feel restless again. He could sense that the tile store was evolving into a mom-and pop-venture, and Erich didn't want to be the brother that came with the building, so he sold them his portion of the business and continued his search.

Eventually, he figured it out. He learned how to use an accounting software program that had been designed for use by huge multinational corporations but that hardly anyone could operate properly. He became a freelance consultant, teaching companies how to use the program and apply it to their unique circumstances. He loved the problem-solving aspect of this work, and he loved the fact that each job lasted just long enough to hold his interest. Between assignments, he satisfied his longing to make things by buying old houses, renovating them himself from top to bottom, and then turning them into rental properties. At last, he found himself in the right place at the right time.

His personal life followed a similar course. His first two marriages had ended in divorce; both times, the relationships seemed to stop growing after only a few years and then go stagnant. Both separations were amicable, and fortunately, no children were involved. Then, not long after Erich began his consulting work, he met another person who had been waiting for a long time to feel truly at home in her own life. Tamiko was a single mother who worked for one of the companies Erich was helping. They kept in touch after Erich had finished the job, started dating, and when they married in 2005 Erich became both a husband and the stepfather to a six-year-old boy named John. Four years later, William was born. With plenty of novelty and challenge at work to keep him satisfied, the stability of domestic life became a welcome piece of the puzzle for Erich. It came at the right time.

The Viking child who once scoffed at art and music now has a house filled with paintings, and he listens to the classical station on the radio when he's driving or putting up drywall. And he has a colicky baby; William is a screamer, just like Erich was. "It must be payback," Erich said, as we made our way back down the hill. "Mom would have enjoyed this."

Just as we got back to the house, Erich's cell phone rang. It was Daniel calling from the hospital. I could hear his voice, and he sounded frantic. He said that something was very wrong; we had to get the girls out of there right away. Erich and I rushed to the hospital, where we found Isabela and Livia, looking frozen with fear, in the waiting room outside the ICU. Erich went in to join Daniel, and I stayed in the waiting room with the girls to keep them company. I gave them some change so they could buy some snacks from a vending machine, but other than that, there wasn't much to distract us. A television bolted to the wall ran continuous advertisements for prescription medicines, mostly for age-related problems. I couldn't think of a thing to say, and I thought it would only make matters worse if I started hugging them or offering to hold their hands. Thankfully, Tamiko arrived only a few minutes later, holding baby William. The girls perked up as soon as they saw their little cousin. Erich eventually came out from the ICU, took me aside, and told me that Rachel was having congestive heart failure. She had nearly gone into cardiac arrest just as Daniel and the girls arrived. He asked if Tamiko and I could take the girls home.

I told Isabela and Livia that the doctors wanted their mommy to rest and that their daddy wanted to keep her company, so the best thing for us to do would be to go out for lunch with Aunt Tamiko and the baby. We all piled into my rental car and drove to Bethel to the girls' favorite restaurant. When we got there it was closed. We kept driving and tried several other restaurants, but all of them were completely booked, with people lined up outside the doors to wait for their tables. It was Sunday brunch on Mother's Day. I should have known.

We drove around for over an hour. The girls were hungry and upset, and who could blame them? They gradually got quiet, and somehow that was worse than when they were arguing. At last we found a pizza place at a mall that could seat us, and I told our server that we needed to order right away. "Happy Mother's Day!" he chirped. I wanted to stuff a breadstick in his mouth.

Tamiko and I struggled to make conversation with the girls while we waited for the pizza. We got them to solve the puzzles on their children's place settings; that kept them busy for a while. I've never felt so grateful to see a box of fucking crayons. We asked them about school, their friends, their hobbies, their favorite animals, their favorite colors, anything we could think of. The food took forty minutes to come.

After lunch, we drove home and watched television all afternoon. Erich called toward the end of the day to report that Rachel was stable for the time being but in bad shape. Dad came in and offered to watch the girls for a while so I could go to the hospital, where Rachel was unconscious and intubated. Daniel sat next to the bed, holding her hand. After an hour or so, I convinced Daniel to come out to the waiting room, where I had some food for him. He couldn't eat. A resident came out to talk to us and, by coincidence, he had immigrated from Romania just like Daniel. The two of them had a brief conversation in Romanian, then the resident asked Daniel to sign a paper giving them permission to insert an arterial blood pressure meter into Rachel's body so they could keep closer track of Rachel's condition. He warned Daniel that this device was risky to use, but he recommended it anyway. "Why?" Daniel asked. "Because your wife's condition is grave," the resident answered. Daniel asked him what he meant by grave—what did that mean?

"Your wife is very, very sick," the resident said. He explained that the infection in Rachel's lungs had already destroyed a significant amount of tissue that could never be recovered.

"What does that mean?" Daniel asked.

"It means one of her lungs is already dead."

That lung would have to be removed surgically to prevent the infection from spreading, but Rachel was too weak for surgery at that point. We could only wait and hope that her immune system and the antibiotics could buy her some time. In the meantime, they were sending out samples to labs all over the country to see if they could identify the virus.

I think that up until that moment, Daniel assumed that Rachel would need a lot of medicine and time to rest, but that she would recover completely. The news that one of her lungs was already lost and that she might not survive the procedure to remove it hit him hard, and the resident's questions about their vacation in Central America—"Did you visit any caves? Was your wife bitten by any animals?"—planted the seed in his mind that all of this was his fault for having organized the trip. When the resident left the room, Daniel started apologizing to me, and his grief was excruciating to witness. I took his hand and told him that this was not his fault and that none of us blamed him for it, but I don't think it brought him any comfort.

I left the hospital, crossed the parking lot, and got into the car, knowing that I would have to drive back to Rachel's house, cook dinner for the girls, and then put them to bed. I would have to do this knowing that their mother might not survive the night. It occurred to me that I didn't know if I could pull it off. What if I started to panic when I was alone with the girls? What would I do then? I couldn't bring myself to start the car. I thought of calling Jessica, but my hands were shaking too hard; I couldn't press the little goddamn buttons on my cell phone, and my vision was blurry, so I couldn't see the numbers anyway. Then I thought, *There's no way out of this,* and that's how I was able to start the car.

I returned to the house and got through it. I made dinner and then shared the family bed with the girls until they fell asleep. I remained there until Daniel came in at around three in the morning with no news. We had some vodka in the kitchen and then Daniel went upstairs to get some sleep. Mother's Day was over.

Fifteen

A RESIDENT FROM THE HOSPITAL called before six the next morning, and Daniel rushed out of the house before I could ask him what was going on. The girls slept through it, thank goodness. My father came into the kitchen looking a thousand years old. He hadn't put his false teeth in yet, and after hearing Daniel's car roar out of the driveway, he was prepared to hear the worst. When I told him that I had no idea what was going on, he turned without a word and went back up to his lonely apartment. I made breakfast for the girls again and got them ready for school. I offered to make pancakes, but they said they actually preferred cereal, so I poured them some Cheerios. Livia, unbeknownst to me, only eats plain Cheerios, and I had put Honey Nut Cheerios into her bowl. She lifted the bowl up and, without a word, tossed it backward, right over her head, against the wall. I didn't feel annoyed at all. It was like watching a stack of books fall over because you've piled it too high. I asked her to help me clean it up and she did, then I gave her the plain Cheerios, and it was as if nothing had happened. She pulled out her homework from the day before and proudly showed me that her teacher had put a star sticker on it. To hell with the Cheerios, I thought. She can toss whatever she wants.

The girls usually waited for the bus at the neighbor's house with their friends, so I walked them over, and after the bus picked them up I called Erich. He was already at the hospital and said that Rachel had had another crisis but was stable again. I drove myself there, and a nurse who was helping out in the ICU that morning talked to Erich and Daniel and me for a while. He said that we mustn't give up hope, that he'd once seen a marathon runner in the ICU with atypical pneumonia who was on a ventilator for a month, and that guy made a full recovery. He said that Rachel's oxygen levels were higher that morning, and that was a good sign. As long as one of the lungs was getting oxygen into her blood, there was hope.

Jessica called me to suggest that I take the girls to the Build-A-Bear store in the mall, since they'd mentioned wanting to go there. I did that after the girls came home from school, and then we had dinner at a restaurant in the food court. Over dinner, the girls had a brief, whispered conference with each other, after which they confided that, when asked to make wishes to put inside their stuffed bears, they had both wished for the same thing: that their mother would come home soon. They took this as a sign that the wish would surely come true.

Daniel got home at around midnight. I woke up at about four to use the bathroom and found him out in the living room, lying on the couch watching television. His eyes were open but he didn't see me. The hospital called before six, so he was out again before the girls woke up.

That day, the doctors decided that they had to get the bad lung out of Rachel's body in spite of the high risk. The infection was killing her. She was drifting in and out of consciousness at that point but was able to give her assent during one of her lucid moments. I stayed at the house with the girls all that day, so I didn't get to see Rachel before she went into surgery. The doctors put together an emergency team and began the procedure late that afternoon. Erich and Daniel kept vigil at the hospital while I made dinner for the girls and watched television with them until bedtime. The waiting was awful. At around eight o'clock, Erich called, and his voice sounded thin. The doctors had opened Rachel's chest cavity, but her blood oxygen levels suddenly dropped so low that she would have died within minutes if they hadn't aborted the procedure. They closed her up and rushed her back to the ICU. Now, she had not only the infection to deal with but all the stress of having had her chest cut open and having gone for some time without sufficient oxygen. She was completely unconscious by then, in a coma.

I put the girls to bed and read a few books to them. Once they'd fallen asleep on either side of me, I found myself thinking that this might be the last time they would be able to close their eyes in that bed and believe that they would see their mother again. I had to think about something else. What was happening to Rachel was awful, but the thought of two little girls losing their mother—that was unbearable.

Sixteen

WHEN I HAD BEEN IN Connecticut for two weeks, Daniel's brother Liviu, who lives in Canada, received an emergency visa and flew down to help. Rachel was still unconscious after the aborted procedure to remove her lung, but her condition had been relatively stable for several days. None of the samples the doctors had sent to labs all over the country matched any known exotic viruses; the doctors said that we just had to hope that her own immune system would rally in time. Rachel was young and otherwise healthy; it wasn't hopeless, the doctors said. With Liviu there, I decided it would be all right for me to fly home for a weekend to see my own girls. Saying good-bye to my nieces wasn't as difficult as I'd feared, partly because they were excited to see Liviu and partly because I would be returning after only a few days. My homecoming wasn't the restorative experience I was hoping it would be, however. The moment I stepped in the door, Ava and Esme delivered the exciting news: Our new dog would arrive the following day!

Oh, yes. The dog. "Yes, girls, I am excited."

The couple from North Carolina who run the kennel showed up in a large van on Friday with their school-age son and four or five dogs to deliver in California, including ours. I made a silent promise to be open-minded about it, but the moment the couple released their snuffling, darting, urinating cargo into our front yard, I knew that this was not going to work for me. Ours was shaggy, white, weighed at least fifty pounds, and looked as dumb as a doorpost. She had one blue eye and one brown one, leading Jessica and the girls to name her "Bowie," after David Bowie, the rock star, who also has different-colored eyes—and whose music I've never liked.

I slunk back into the house, lay down on my bed, put a pillow over my face, and screamed. I could see my fate as clearly as if it were appearing in a crystal ball: I would feel uncomfortable in my own house for the next dozen years. I could have said no to this, but I didn't. I didn't want to be the kind of dad who wouldn't let his kids have a dog. Now I would be the kind of dad who wished his kids' dog would hurry up and croak.

The van full of dogs disappeared after a couple of hours. To my relief, they took Bowie with them—they like to give the animals a chance to get used to their new homes gradually. The whole traveling kennel stayed at a nearby motel for the night. I took the girls with me to go grocery shopping, but all they could talk about was the dog. The traffic in the parking lot seemed worse than usual, and the shoppers in the store all seemed to be in a rush, jostling for position in the aisles as if we were all in some sort of Roman chariot race. Half of them were talking on their cell phones, and my girls kept asking me if I loved Bowie, because I didn't seem that excited about it. Why wasn't I more excited? Didn't I love Bowie?

"Yes, I love Bowie."

Meanwhile, I had to decide what to cook for dinner, and I couldn't think of a thing. The choice of foods was overwhelming, yet nothing appealed to me, and for a moment I considered walking out of the store without anything and just going home. But the thought of having to get in the car again an hour or two later to have dinner at a restaurant didn't appeal to me, so I grabbed some frozen pot stickers and a bunch of broccoli, let the girls buy some gum, and got the hell out of there as fast as I could.

I went to bed right after dinner, at around seven o'clock. I woke up at midnight and couldn't fall asleep again for the rest of the night.

The dog people returned on Saturday for a second meet and greet. They showed us the commands and gave us all sorts of advice about how to care for the dog. I couldn't keep track of any of this; it was all just noise to me. Then they left Bowie with us—the transfer was complete. She was our dog now. We offered her food but she refused to eat, and she wouldn't poop in her "potty spot." She crapped in the girls' sandbox instead, and she had diarrhea. Jessica explained that the stress of travel and of being in unfamiliar surroundings affects dogs strongly. That night, we put her into her crate—she was supposedly crate-trained—and she howled and whined and barked miserably and scratched at the metal bars so desperately that I thought she would tear her nails right out of her paws. The trainers had given us a plastic milk jug with some BBs in it and told us to shake it if she made too much noise. We tried that, but it didn't work.

Then, on Sunday, the trainers came back again with four other dogs to do some filming. Jessica had made a barter arrangement with them—we got a discount on the fee for training the dog, and in return, Jessica promised to shoot some footage showing what they do. The owners of two other dogs that this couple had delivered on previous visits to L.A. came to our house with their dogs so that Jessica could show them interacting with their pets and interview them. So we had dogs and dog people and cameras around the house all day. I stayed indoors the whole time; it was just too much. Dog this, dog that, dog dog dog. Daddy could have used some of that attention after the two weeks he'd just had, but Daddy didn't have fur or a tail, so he was going to have to wait his turn.

After the filming was done and the crowd cleared out, having only one snuffling quadruped in the house didn't seem so bad, but then we went through the nighttime ordeal of the howling and the whining and the barking and the scratching again, and having just one seemed plenty bad enough.

Early the next morning, as I packed my suitcase for my return to Connecticut, Erich called with unexpected news. The doctor overseeing Rachel's case had sat down with him and Daniel and spent a full hour answering their questions, and he actually sounded optimistic. At the end of their meeting, he said, "She will walk out of here on her own two feet."

When I hung up the phone, I immediately pictured the scene in my mind: Rachel appearing in the doorway to her house, her daughters rushing to greet her. I went to tell Jessica the good news, and on the way through the living room I stepped in something wet. Our pretrained adult dog had pissed on the floor. I mopped it up and resumed packing.

Seventeen

THE FLIGHT BACK TO CONNECTICUT seemed to take forever. My connection to White Plains was delayed four hours, so I got on a plane to Hartford instead. Erich and Dad came to pick me up there. Erich's car window was broken; it wouldn't close all the way, so we could barely hear each other over the sound of the wind rushing into the car. None of us felt like talking anyway. By the time Erich and Dad dropped me off at Daniel's house, the girls were already asleep. Daniel thanked me for coming, then he drove immediately to the hospital, and I didn't hear when he came back.

The next day, Rachel's condition worsened, and the doctors decided they had to open her up again to remove her infected lung or she wouldn't survive the night. It was very tense. I stayed at the house with the girls, playing board games with them in the living room, while Erich called me every hour from outside the operating room. Neither of us thought Rachel would make it. Somehow, she did. They got the lung out, but after the operation, the doctor who guaranteed Rachel would walk out of the hospital on her own two feet was nowhere to be seen. A different doctor advised Daniel and Erich that the amount of oxygen getting to Rachel's brain had dropped so low during the procedure that there was a chance that if Rachel did survive, she might not be the same person we knew. They posted a full-time nurse in Rachel's room in the ICU after that, because her condition was so bad.

I went to see Rachel the next morning, and what I saw broke my heart. One of her eyes was open, and I looked into it. It was like staring into a fish's eye at the market.

Lisa, Rachel's neighbor, offered to watch Isabela and Livia all afternoon, so Erich and I took a long walk in the woods. We were of one mind—the worst-case scenario was no longer that Rachel might die, it was that she would be kept alive as a vegetable, thanks to the miracle of modern fucking medicine, in a nursing home. And her husband and daughters would be expected to feel grateful for this miracle. They would be obliged to visit her living corpse on weekends and holidays, and this "miracle" would ruin them. They would lose their home and who knows what else. That, we agreed, would be a fate worse than death.

We got this talk out of our system and went back to Rachel's house to have dinner. Daniel was there, and he fired up his big outdoor oven. He got that oven so hot it could have melted lead. He and Erich roasted a rack of lamb, short ribs, a duck, and a huge platter of vegetables in olive oil. I don't even know how many bottles of wine we drank. Then I remembered that I'd promised to do a shift at the hospital that night so that Daniel could stay home with the girls. The thought of how bad it would be if I got in an accident definitely got my adrenaline going, and man, did I drive carefully! I sat my ass down in the chair next to Rachel's bed, and then I got dizzy. To stay awake, I decided to write a letter to Rachel, in case she recovered, so she would have some idea of what a night in the ICU had been like for her unconscious body.

Hi Rachel. It's seven at night and I'm in your room in the ICU. I told Daniel and Erich that I would stay here tonight, and I promised to call them in an emergency, but I'm determined not to do that unless I have to.

I thought I might try putting together a little record of what's going on so that if you somehow make it through this ordeal, you can get a picture of it from this side of the ventilator tube.

Right now, a pair of nurses are sticking you with a needle to take a blood sample. Two minutes ago another nurse was in here to take a blood sample and she got it through your arterial shunt, which doesn't require a new needle. But now they are using a needle. So I asked why and they said they need to take a sample "peripherally," whatever that means. Every few minutes, someone is poking you with a new hole. Fortunately, you don't seem to be feeling any pain.

I wonder how much of this you will remember. Not much, I hope. Hopefully, and I haven't lost hope, you will pull through. If you are reading this, then you did pull through and it will surely seem odd to be reading this. Erich and I were saying today that, for the last eight days, whenever a fork in the road came where you could either begin to improve or get worse, your condition took the turn for the worse. And each day it seemed that you had reached a point so catastrophic that the only way it could get worse was for you to die. But no—it always turned out that you could get worse and still be alive. I don't understand how your body has tolerated what it has been through. Last night's botched operation was only—

Sorry. The nurses asked me to step out while they rubbed you with lotion. Your temperature is up to 103—they say if it doesn't go down soon, I may have to call Daniel, because it may be the sign of a final crisis. I'm not going to do it yet. Forgive me Rachel, but those girls need him, for a few hours at least.

The nurses are giving you lots of Tylenol intravenously and are using plenty of cooling blankets to try to control the fever. The one looking after you at the moment has three young children. Her husband is a stay-at-home dad like me. She just told me that the nurses here love you because you've been so sweet, so uncomplaining. You even apologized to one of them for having to ask for help when your period started. They are all praying for you.

Every few minutes an alarm goes off in your room, one of the five or six machines keeping you alive. Very loud alarms, I suppose to get the nurses' attention. But it must be disturbing to you even if you're unconscious. How can your body rest through all this?

Now two nurses are here to check on something else. One crisis after another. It's only 8:30. In ninety minutes, you've nearly died several times. Your blood pressure is dropping right now. The nurse said I might start thinking about calling Daniel. I asked if I could hold off for just fifteen minutes more and they said yes.

They've asked me to leave while they deal with the crisis. Please hang in there. The thing about these crises is that they—

I forgot what I was going to write. I suppose it was something about how those crises get my adrenaline going and then my thinking gets very confused.

I'm in the waiting room only a few yards away from you. So many alarms are going off. Are they all for you?

It's 9:05, and every minute that passes without someone telling me I have to call Daniel is another minute that he's at home. The girls will be asleep soon. Earlier today I was thinking that tonight would be a long night, but now I hope it is a long night, I hope it seems an endless night, as long as no one tells me I have to make that phone call. But every time someone walks near this room, each footstep makes a little explosion go off in my chest.

Tonight one of the nurses told me she gets panic attacks! Small world. She said to the other nurse, "It makes you feel that you are dying." That's pretty accurate.

Sweet Rachel, you're doing all the work in there.

9:50

They called me back in and your blood pressure is back up and your temperature is down. There's a machine cooling you off now. There sure are a lot of machines working on you—I can't even count them because I don't know where one ends and the other begins.

Erich called while I was out in the waiting room, and I gave him a full report and we agreed that I should call him back only if there was

103

an "issue" once the nurses had called me back in. The nurses seem calm, and your numbers look good. But the night isn't over yet.

I'm looking at you now, and I'm imagining you getting up, taking that tube out of your mouth, and saying, "OK, time for a gin and tonic." For some reason, today I've had several waves of feeling, a sense that you will recover.

Another alarm. Now what? What is really going on in your body?

The nurses were saying tonight that every year they get a few cases of extremely severe pneumonia in young women, and one said, "I don't know why it's always young women," and the other said, "I do. It's because women are trying to do so much, juggling work and taking care of their kids, and housework. They feel like they have to do it all, and they don't give themselves any break."

Tamiko was saying this about you the other day. She said you work yourself way too hard, and Erich agreed. They both said that you seem tired all the time. I don't see you often enough to have an opinion on this.

10:04

No one came in after the alarm, so I guess it wasn't bad. It's really hard to concentrate in here.

Right now I'm thinking about a dish I want to make for dinner tomorrow. I think even Livia will eat it. I suppose that this is my coping strategy. I'm occupying myself with thoughts about things I can do, like the idea for tonight's dinner. Did I describe it for you? I got this brainstorm that I could convince Daniel to come home at a regular dinnertime, eat with the girls, watch a movie with them, and then go to sleep with them. To my surprise, he agreed. The agreement was that I would stay here and call if anything went wrong. So I cooked beef Stroganoff, broccoli, egg noodles, and had it all ready by the time Daniel made it home. The girls were so excited. When they saw his car in the driveway they ran out squealing with delight, and Daniel looked just as happy.

I had prepped Dad by saying that if I had to call Daniel, he should be ready to come over and sleep in the guest room so that someone was there with the girls.

By the way, that's what we had to do the night when the doctors tried the surgery to remove the infected lung. Erich and Daniel were with you all day, and then the surgery supposedly began at 7:30, but at 10:30 the doctors told Daniel and Erich that it had been unsuccessful. It was crushing to us all, and I sensed that Erich and Daniel would be unable to leave the hospital at all that night, so I decided I had to convince them it was OK to leave for a few hours. Daniel especially was almost delirious from exhaustion. So I called Dad, knowing he would think it was to say that you had not survived the operation. But he stayed calm and I explained what he needed to do, and he walked over with his teeth in a cup and went to bed in the downstairs room and off I went. I was able to convince Erich to leave at 1:30 and Daniel at 2:30. I went home just before dawn and Daniel was already up, warming some food in the microwave.

It's 10:30 now and nothing bad is happening. I wish I'd been smart enough to pack my reading glasses for this trip. My eyelids are getting heavy. I didn't sleep at all last night. Dad and Erich and Daniel and I had lunch at a Portuguese restaurant called Atlantico today, after you'd had another crisis and then stabled out again. We left the hospital feeling grim, but after a few glasses of wine we were actually able to have a few laughs. The bottle of wine the waitress recommended to us was named "EA." It was a Portuguese wine. We decided that "EA" must be the word that Portuguese people utter right before they die, and somehow, at the time, it seemed very funny.

My concentration is flagging. I thought half an hour had passed but it's only 10:40. Well, earlier I said I hoped the night would seem endless because of the anticipation of bad news that never came, so I'm trying to remind myself right now to be grateful.

Now it's 11:10. Feels like hours have passed, like being stuck on a long flight in an uncomfortable plane seat. Nothing bad is happening right now. I asked the nurse if she has gotten to the point where she no longer feels nervous when the alarms go off and she said, "Oh, no. I pray every day, all day, here at work."

I told the nurse that I was keeping a record of your journey for you, and she winced. "Do you really think she'd want to see that?" she asked. Now I'm not so sure it's a good idea.

In the meantime, they're rubbing you down again and so I have to step out to the waiting room. Just a few minutes ago, a respiratory technician walked in and introduced herself and explained that she had taken you down here from your regular room last week. She took one look at you and was unable to disguise how shocked she felt. "I didn't leave her like this," she said.

11:45

Everything was going well; then the nurse injected you with something and an alarm went off. She started tipping the bed up and down, and then she yelled to another nurse, "Call the resident." And then she told me I had to leave.

I'm out here in the waiting room again. I'll just brace and wait.

12:15

The nurse came out and told me things were calm again. I'm back in your room. Your heart rate and blood pressure had suddenly dropped. My vision is too blurry to keep writing, I'm sorry.

4:45

I must have dozed off in the chair for a few hours. The nurse said that you'd been stable the whole time. I'm going to leave. I gave the nurse my cell number and told her that if any crisis developed to please call my number first so I could go upstairs and wake Daniel up gently rather than have him and the girls get awakened by the phone ringing.

Eighteen

THAT SUNDAY, MAY 24, was Isabela's ninth birthday—and my daughter Esme's fifth. I called home to wish Esme a happy birthday. Meanwhile, Rachel had planned a birthday party for Isabela, but in order to schedule a visit from an animal group that entertains at parties with lizards and giant toads and all, the party had been set for the following weekend. For Isabela's actual birthday, Erich offered to have us all over to his place for dinner. He planned to barbecue something for us if it stopped raining.

Daniel got a call from the hospital before seven that morning and rushed out. Dad walked over from his garage apartment to give Isabela a birthday present. He'd bought her a kit that comes with a pair of flip-flops and some paints and glue and appliqué stuff so the flip-flops could be customized. Isabela pulled them out of the box and right away you could see they were way too big for her; they were adult-size. But Isabela, bless her heart, didn't give any sign of being disappointed. Without missing a beat, she said to her sister, "Livia, let's make them for Mom when she comes home!" So they did. It was too much for Dad to watch; he went back to his apartment.

I made butterscotch chip pancakes for the girls, but they didn't like them, so we settled on eggs and toast. Livia seemed very angry that day. I gave Isabela and Livia the gifts and goodie bags that Jessica had chosen for them and sent with me, and Livia was glad to have something to open. It rained all morning, and we had a lot of thunder.

When afternoon came, it was still very dark and gloomy, and I had a headache that wouldn't go away no matter how many pills I swallowed. The girls watched TV. Erich was at the hospital, and he called to say Rachel had developed a secondary viral infection in the other lung. Because she was not getting enough oxygen, the doctors had injected her with a paralyzing drug to shut the rest of her body down and conserve energy. This prompted Dad to wonder if the doctors were aware that Rachel had been taking antidepressants up until the day she'd been admitted to the hospital. He left a message with Rachel's psychiatrist's answering service, and a few minutes later the psychiatrist called back to say that yes, the doctors should definitely be informed. Rachel was on two antidepressants simultaneously and, in addition, had been taking Xanax four times a day to cope with anxiety.

We called the nursing station at the hospital, hoping we might have stumbled upon the key to Rachel's recovery, but it turned out that Rachel had provided all this information the day she had checked in.

The rain eased up, and we had the barbecue over at Erich's. There were a lot of people there. I felt tired, and my head was pounding the whole time. I went out onto the porch, thinking I would be by myself, but it turned out I had company. It was Livia. I said hello but she didn't answer. She was staring out toward the woods, all six years and fifty pounds of her, light brown curls, green eyes just like her mother's. In profile she looks exactly like Rachel; the resemblance is haunting. I sat down in the rocking chair, and we were quiet for a while. Suddenly, Livia turned her face up toward the sky, clenched her fists, and yelled with all her might, "Dear Mommy, I miss you! Love, Livia!"

I felt like I'd been stabbed with an ice pick. I said good night to everybody, drove back to Rachel's house, and went to bed.

The next day, Daniel came back from the hospital before lunch and announced that it was time for a break: He wanted to take all of us to Norwalk for lunch and a visit to the aquarium. Dad came along too. We watched an IMAX movie about a stretch of ocean off the east coast of Africa. It was just what I needed to see—images of nature without any narrative or moral commentary. No melodrama, just spectacle. Awe rather than agitation.

That night at dinner, I encouraged Daniel to talk about his childhood in Romania, and he told some good stories. Seeing the way his daughters looked at him while he talked was very touching. I found myself thinking that if Rachel didn't make it, the girls might be OK, with the father they've got. And then I felt guilty for thinking that.

Daniel put the girls to bed while I did the dishes. At 9:30, the phone rang. I answered. It was a resident from the hospital. Rachel's heart rate was dropping; they were about to do CPR. I had to tell Daniel, and he rushed out without a word. I went upstairs and read a couple of books to the girls. I spent the whole night with them—Daniel didn't return from the hospital until after dawn. At 4:00 a.m. Livia woke up screaming, then she said she was hungry and wanted Cheerios. I hesitated for a moment, and she started screaming again, so I went downstairs and fixed the cereal for her. Isabela said, "I know it's late, but could you read to us again? I don't think we're going to be able to sleep anymore." I turned on the lights and we read more books.

Daniel came back at six thirty to take a shower and change his clothes. He said that Rachel's weight was up from 120 pounds to 190 because her body was swelling up with fluid. The drugs that would make the fluid drain out of her affected her heart adversely, so they couldn't give them to her anymore. She wasn't getting any nutrition—any protein—which meant the fluid wasn't being absorbed in her body, so even though she was filled with water, she was completely dehydrated. One of many concerns at that point was that her bladder might burst.

That day happened to be Ava's birthday—my daughters' birthdays are only two days apart. As I had done with Esme, I called Ava to wish her a happy birthday and apologized for not being there. She sounded as cheerful as ever. She asked me, "How is your sister?" and I had a hard time thinking of what to say, so I changed the subject.

The next day, Rachel weighed 206 pounds and her kidneys had failed. She didn't look real at all; she looked like a wax museum figure. The doctors started her on dialysis to remove the toxins from her blood, but they warned us that she might not be able to tolerate the procedure in her condition.

Twenty-four hours later, a doctor informed us that Rachel's liver had been irreparably damaged. But then he said that the dialysis seemed to be working, and her vital levels were rising. This planted the idea in Daniel's mind that Rachel would survive. He was certain of it.

My father and I had a long talk about what to do if it looked like Rachel could be kept alive indefinitely but in a vegetative state. We agreed that that must not happen. If either of us were in that condition, we would want our spouses to pull the plug. But how did Daniel feel? We didn't know, and we didn't know how or when to bring it up with him. At that point, he seemed sure that Rachel would recover. And what about the girls? When would the time come to prepare them for all this? Up until then, Daniel had insisted that they be shielded from the full gravity of the situation. Mommy was sick and the doctors were taking care of her and she would get well; that was what he had been telling them all along, and it seemed like as good an idea as any to me.

I suggested that we call Rachel's psychiatrist to ask if he had any suggestions for how to handle this. You might think that my father, given his bias against psychotherapy, would have balked at this suggestion, but he didn't. He trusted this particular psychiatrist, and with good reason: Rachel had convinced our dad to give this doctor—and medication—a try, and his experience with antidepressant medication was positive. "If only they'd had these drugs fifty years ago," Dad lamented, after he'd found the combination that worked for him. "I might have painted happy clowns on velvet and made a living at it."

Dad called the psychiatrist, and he agreed to see us right away. He hadn't known about Rachel's illness before getting my father's message, and he looked stricken when we described her condition. We asked him if there was anything we could be doing to help Isabela and Livia through this. Should we be encouraging them to talk about what they were feeling, or just leave them alone? Was there anything we should especially avoid doing?

He didn't pretend to have all the answers, and I liked that about him. Under circumstances like these, he said, simply being there for the girls and playing it by ear was probably the best anyone could do. But then he took the conversation in an unexpected direction. He suggested to my dad that he needed to step up and become more of a father figure to Daniel. Right away.

"You're Rachel's father; you're the paterfamilias, he'll listen to you." He recommended that Dad let Daniel know how we felt about keeping Rachel alive if she were truly brain dead. He also recommended that we encourage Daniel to tell the girls that their mother might not recover, because if she died before he had prepared them in some way, they might feel that they'd been deceived.

My father listened attentively, but I found it difficult to imagine him suddenly taking on the paterfamilias role. Still, I was impressed by the way the doctor had handled our meeting. I decided that if I ever had trouble with panic attacks again, I would call him.

Later in the afternoon, I met with the director of a grief counseling center in Danbury that offers various kinds of support to families, especially children who have lost a parent. I asked him what we should do about Isabela's birthday party that Sunday if

Rachel died before then. Should we cancel it? He said, "Ask the child. If the child wants to have the party, have the party and don't make her feel guilty for wanting it. So much is being taken away from her; if she wants something that she's looked forward to for a long time, let her have that. If she says she would rather not have the party, then cancel it and don't make her feel guilty for not wanting to celebrate."

That seemed like sound advice. But if Rachel died, I didn't know how we would pull that off, with a house full of kids and lizards and horned toads and god knows what else that outfit was supposed to bring. How do you sing "Happy Birthday" to a girl whose mother just died? I truly did not want to find out the answer to that question.

So much was going to change. Daniel was going to need a lot of help. It was good to know that there was a place he could go to ask for it. The center offered help with everything from counseling to recommendations for temporary childcare and housecleaning services. I wouldn't be able to stay in Connecticut forever, and Dad told me that as soon as this was over, he was going to move back to Arizona. He couldn't stay in that garage apartment anymore— Rachel's ghost would haunt him.

The next day was Saturday, May 30. Daniel was home, and Dad came over to join us for breakfast. After we'd eaten, Isabela and Livia asked if they could go across the street to where one of their friends was having a tag sale. I walked them over and chatted with the friend's mom, Annie. She offered to watch the girls for the rest of the morning to give me a break.

I went back into the house. Dad was still sitting at the table, when he turned to Daniel and said, in a very matter-of-fact way, that we needed to talk about Rachel. He said that none of us wanted Rachel to live like a vegetable and that it was time to get a neurologist to examine her. "If she's brain dead," he said calmly but firmly, "we've got to turn off the machines. We'll do it together, all of us. It won't be just you."

At first I couldn't tell what Daniel was thinking. He was quiet, looking at the table. Then he started to cry and he said, "No, Grandpa—don't say that." Dad got up and hugged him, and Daniel wept silently in his arms for a few moments, then they both sat back down. Dad said, "And you've got to prepare the girls before that happens."

"When?" Daniel asked.

"Now."

Daniel stood up, went to the front screen door, and called out to the girls. "I need you to come here. Daddy needs to talk to you."

This was it—this was what I most feared. Having to be present at the moment when those girls learned that they would never see their mother again.

The girls came in and Daniel had them sit next to him at the dining room table. He reached out to touch their hands and he said, "There is something I have to tell you. The doctors have done everything they can to help Mommy, and Mommy has done everything she can to get better, but the sickness she got is too strong. She may not get better. She may not come home."

His voice broke, but he managed to keep going. "But I want to make sure you understand something. It's not because she wanted to leave us. She tried so hard to come back to us, so very hard. It's not anyone's fault. It's not your fault, it's not her fault. Mommy loves you very much. Do you understand?"

Isabela started to cry. Livia picked up a little ball and wrapped it in a white tablecloth and began moving it across the table, like a little ghost, and she made the sound a ghost makes: "*Whooooooo . . .*"

"Do you understand what Daddy is telling you, Livia? Do you understand that Mommy loves you? I need for you to tell me that you understand that."

Livia nodded.

"It's not fair," Isabela said through tears.

"No, it isn't," Daniel said. "But Mommy loves you, she will always love you, and I will always love you, and I'm not going anywhere. I'm not going to leave you. And I don't want either of you to worry that you might get sick and die. This is something very rare. Not even the doctors know what it is. If you girls get a cold, I don't want you thinking you're going to die. Do you understand what Daddy is telling you?"

The girls nodded.

Daniel hugged them and kissed them and then asked if they had any questions. Isabela, looking very determined, asked, "Can we go back now? Across the street."

"Yes," Daniel said, and he let them go, and they walked out the front door.

Daniel asked me if I would follow the girls and watch them to make sure that they were OK. Then he called Erich and said to meet him at the hospital. It was time to find a neurologist.

I walked across the street, and Annie offered me a lawn chair to sit on while I watched the girls. I was still trying to digest what I'd just seen and heard: my father, behaving not at all like a rabbit; Daniel delivering the awful news to his children with perfect simplicity and tenderness; the girls, absorbing only as much of the news as they could bear and then seeking refuge in the distraction of the tag sale. I watched in awe as they helped their friend draw up little price tags for the old toys. Isabela made a large notice advertising the sale and asked if I would walk up the street to help her attach it to a stop sign. As we walked up the long hill, she asked me if Ava and Esme ever had tag sales, and if I had ever held one when I was a kid. She seemed to want to talk about tag sales only, so I followed her lead, and that was our conversation as we taped up the notice and walked back down to the neighbor's house. I bought a few dolls for my kids, which delighted Isabela and Livia, and when another neighbor stopped by and bought a few things, they were just as excited.

I stayed at the tag sale for an hour or so, and then Dad came over. "Erich just called from the hospital," he said. "It's time."

I asked Annie if she could watch the girls, and she said she'd be glad to—she'd give them lunch too. I stopped by the neighbor Lisa's house and told her what was going on, and she said she could take the girls all afternoon and all evening if necessary. I pulled Rachel's car out of the garage, Dad got in, and we drove to the hospital. We didn't say anything to each other on the way. Just as we were parking, my cell phone rang. It was Erich, asking us to hurry. We stepped out of the car, and Dad suddenly clutched his left arm against his body with his right hand and started running. I caught up with him, and we rode the elevator up to the ICU floor. As soon as it opened, Dad ran past the nursing station to Rachel's room.

Erich and Daniel were on either side of the bed. Erich was holding Rachel's good hand (the other had turned completely black from the arterial pressure monitor), and Daniel was stroking her forehead. Rachel looked ghastly. She was still swollen—her neck was wider than her head, and it didn't look real at all—and still intubated, and one of her unseeing eyes was half open. Erich explained to us that the neurologist had examined her and confirmed that she was gone. She'd probably been that way since the first attempted operation. The subsequent operation, all the procedures, all the machines and drugs and alarms and phone calls and crises—they were probably all for nothing. A technician came into the room and Erich said to him, "We're all here now."

The technician called a nurse over, and she explained that she would be giving Rachel an injection of something to prevent muscle spasms. Those spasms would give the false appearance that Rachel was struggling to breathe once the tube had been removed. "This is for the family, really, not for the patient," she said. "The spasms are pure reflex; they aren't a sign that she's conscious. The drug will help her muscles relax until her heart stops. It's more peaceful that way." The technician advised us to step outside for a moment while he and the nurse removed the tube that was doing the breathing for her. "You don't want to see that," he said, and he didn't have to ask us twice. The four of us stepped behind a screen and tried not to listen to the gurgling sounds coming from inside the room. We didn't talk. I felt as if I were standing inside a virtual body rather than a real one. My physical senses were heightened, but I felt no emotion at all. If I could have projected the contents of my consciousness onto a screen, the images would have been unrecognizable.

The technician called us back in, and there was Rachel, without any wires or tubes connected to her. Her lips were bluish purple and her lower lip was misshapen from where the tube had rested for so long. Her eyes were still half open. The four of us surrounded her bed and placed our hands on her arms, her face, her legs, and her feet. There was nothing to do, nothing to hope for, nothing to expect. The nurse returned and used a stethoscope to check for a pulse. She nodded to us and it was done.

"The worst day in my life has come," Daniel said.

I kept my hand on Rachel's foot, but I looked out the window at the puffy white clouds and blue sky and the hills rolling south toward Long Island Sound, and a strange thing happened. I heard a voice say, "The peace of green fields." I heard the voice clearly, but a quick glance around the room confirmed that I was hallucinating. I didn't recognize the phrase; it meant nothing to me.

Dad stood up and said, "I can't stay here anymore," and he walked out. I told Erich and Daniel that I would take him home. I kissed Rachel good-bye and followed Dad out to the parking lot. We got into the car, but I didn't feel like starting it yet. It was windy out—the gusts were so strong they rocked the car. Dad was still clutching his left arm against his chest with his right hand. Was he having a heart attack? I figured he would tell me if anything was wrong. Or maybe he wouldn't. What did it matter, after what he'd just seen? Rachel was his only daughter. If I had to watch one of my girls die, I'd be grateful for a heart attack. He was staring out the window at the valley beyond the hospital. Then he spoke, and he sounded angry.

"Life is bullshit."

Then he turned his face away so I couldn't see him.

At that moment, I asked myself: *If there was a button I could press, and I knew that pressing it would make every human being on the planet disappear instantly, painlessly, forever, without a trace, so that the whole bonfire of fear and hope and confusion and pain would be over with, once and for all—would I press it?* My own children, I reminded myself, would dissolve along with everyone else. Everything dear to me, and everything dear to everyone else would disappear. So would beauty, courage, love, tenderness, curiosity, ambition, art, science, technology, history, knowledge, consciousness—all of it would be erased. Would I press that button?

God yes, I thought. *I would press it in a heartbeat.* And I felt truly sorry that no such button existed.

As soon as we got back home, Dad went upstairs to his apartment. Daniel pulled into the driveway not long after us. I went across the street to fetch the girls. Daniel sat them down again at the dinner table and told them that it was over: Mommy was no longer suffering. Once again, they seemed too shocked to really grasp it all at once. Within minutes, friends of Rachel's and Daniel's started appearing at the house. It was amazing how quickly it happened. Within an hour, we must have had two dozen people there. I felt a strong urge to keep busy, so I started making food for everyone. I made enough dinner to feed forty or fifty people, and that's pretty much how many we had there by late afternoon. Isabela and Livia started a soccer game with the neighbors' kids in the backyard, and when Daniel saw this, he joined them. A few of his soccer buddies followed suit, and before long there was a crazy game going on. Most of the men playing had either wine glasses or beer bottles in their hands, the girls were squealing with delight, and it was as beautiful as it was heartbreaking.

I went over to check on Dad. He was lying on his couch listening to classical music on the radio. "Are you OK?" I asked.

He said, "I tried to stick my head in the oven, but my head wouldn't fit." I truly don't know if he meant it.

There was something I wanted to tell him, about how he'd handled the talk with Daniel that morning. I tried, but I couldn't get my mouth to work. It was very strange, like in dreams where you want to speak or run or look over your shoulder but your body will not obey your mind. I threw up my hands, found a piece of paper and a pen, and wrote: *I have never been so proud of you.* I passed it over to him and he read it and said, "Daniel's the one who had the hard job. I don't know how he did it."

I returned to the house to keep an eye on the food. Dad eventually joined us for dinner, and then he and Erich and I sat out on the porch in front of Rachel's house, where it was quiet. It was a beautiful summer night. None of us could think of anything to say. Then I remembered where the phrase "the peace of green fields" came from: the Marcus Aurelius book on Rachel's bookshelf.[1]

The next morning, Daniel came into the kitchen while I was making breakfast. He opened the medicine cabinet to get some aspirin and saw all the bottles of children's pain relievers and children's cold medicines and children's allergy medicines, and he went pale. He said to me, "What will I do if the girls get sick? Rachel always handled that stuff."

When Isabela came downstairs, Daniel followed the grief counselor's advice and asked her if she° still wanted her birthday party to take place that day. Isabela's answer was a very firm yes, she definitely wanted the party. So we mobilized.

After breakfast I mowed the lawn. Lisa and Annie and at least half a dozen of Rachel's girlfriends came over to help set up. They held a meeting at the table in the backyard and soon they had it all figured out: who would bring napkins, who would bring cups and

---

1 "Let it be clear to you that the peace of green fields can always be yours, in this, that, or any other spot; and that nothing is any different here from what it would be either up in the hills, or down by the sea, or wherever else you will."

paper plates, who would put out balloons, who would go pick up the ice cream cake. Daniel had promised Isabela that he would let all the guests make their own pizza in the big pizza oven, and he wasn't going to go back on his word, so he started chopping wood and getting the dough ready. At one o'clock, the guests started coming, and here came the tricky part: Rachel's illness had come on so suddenly that most of the children who had been invited— and their parents—didn't even know she'd been sick, much less that she had died. None of us had been thinking clearly enough to try to contact the families beforehand to alert them to what was going on, and now it was too late for that, so Annie and I took turns standing at the end of the driveway, waiting for each child and parent to arrive, and then informing them that we had very sad, very shocking news. One by one, the mothers' faces went pale as they placed their hands on their daughters' shoulders and pulled them in close. The little girls stood very still in their party dresses, eyes wide with fear. We explained that Isabela was eager to have something to look forward to on this terrible day, and we hoped everyone would be able to stay for the party, but would understand if they couldn't. Every one of them stayed.

As I did this, once again I felt as if my mind had been planted inside a virtual body. My physical sensations felt real, but nothing else did.

Having that party turned out to be the best thing we could possibly have done. The animal presenters showed up with their civets and armadillos and snakes, and they even had a frog-jumping contest inside the house. The kids had a great time. Daniel helped them make their little pizzas, and then he made a bunch of big ones for the parents. He was obviously relieved to have something to do, something that brought pleasure to others.

I stayed on one more week to help prepare for the memorial service on Friday night. Daniel asked if I would lead the service and deliver the eulogy. I couldn't stop fussing over it until the moment the time came to speak. I was even crossing things out and scribbling in the margins at the funeral home. The toilet stall in the men's room became my office.

Hundreds of people came to the service; it was standing room only in the funeral home. Isabela and Livia begged not to have to attend the event. Daniel felt conflicted about this, so he and I paid another visit to the grief center and asked about it. The counselor there thought that it might do more harm than good to force the kids to go against their will, so Daniel let them stay home while Annie and her daughter kept them company. At the last minute, my father decided not to come either. He said he just couldn't face all those people and have to talk to them about Rachel. He was seventy-nine, and he'd lost his wife six years earlier and now this. I didn't try to change his mind.

Jessica and I talked about her bringing Ava and Esme out for the service, but we decided that it might be better for everyone if, instead, we offered to fly Daniel, Isabela, and Livia to California whenever they felt like getting away. That way, the cousins could see each other under better circumstances. I ran this idea by Daniel, and he liked it very much.

After the service, at least a hundred of us spilled across the street to a restaurant. We turned out to be a noisy bunch. Jessica's father, John, who had flown out from San Francisco for the service, had to stay to the bitter end of the party because I was his ride back to his hotel, but he was a good sport about it, and several people went out of their way to tell me how lucky I was to have such a great father-in-law. Although he complains of having to search for words all the time, if you didn't know he'd had a stroke eight years ago, you wouldn't guess it. He charmed everyone to such an extent that even friends of Rachel's and Erich's that I'd never met were plying him with drinks. After Erich and I paid the bill, we said good night to each other, and John and I went back to the funeral home parking lot. We got into Rachel's car—and the goddamned thing wouldn't start. I managed to flag someone down who had jumper cables, and we set them up, but the engine wouldn't respond. It was truly dead. I had to call Erich at midnight and get him to come for us.

The day after the service, I drove John to Westchester airport, then I drove Liviu and his family to La Guardia. The traffic heading back to New England was awful—it took me five hours to get back—but I didn't mind. I was glad to be by myself. Daniel and the girls and I had dinner at home, and at around nine o'clock that night, Erich came to pick me up. It was time to say good bye. I offered to put the girls to bed and read them one more story, but Isabela, looking and sounding a lot older than nine, said, "It's pretty late, Uncle Mark. You can read to us next time we see each other." I kissed them good night and came downstairs and hugged Daniel, and that's when I fell apart. I felt I was abandoning them, and I couldn't think of anything to say or do to make it better. Erich told me later that the girls, hearing me get so upset, crawled out of bed and were lying on their stomachs, watching us from the top of the stairs. He overheard Livia whisper to Isabela, "Everybody misses Mommy."

I went next door to Dad's apartment, and he thanked me for coming out and helping watch the girls. I told him how badly I felt about leaving, and he said, "You've got your own family; you have to go." He made a shooing gesture so that I could leave. Neither of us wanted to draw it out.

Nineteen

JESSICA AND THE GIRLS PICKED me up at the airport, and I couldn't keep my eyes off them the whole drive home. It was June 6, a month and a day after I'd left. Ava's birthday party had taken place the same day as Isabela's, only instead of a reptile and amphibian show, Ava's party featured an actor made up to look like the wizard Dumbledore from the Harry Potter movies. I got to hear all about it, and I savored every detail. There had been no subtext of tragedy, no agonizing poignancy to their wizard-themed party, nor had grief marred Esme's "Animals and Rainbows"–themed party the week before. We got to the house, I stepped out of the car, and can you guess who rushed forward to greet me?

A barking dog.

Bowie had settled in to her new home while I was away. She stood ready to defend her territory against intruders, and as far as she was concerned, I was an intruder. Her reaction upon seeing me was to explode into desperate, ear-splitting alarm barks and to scurry back and forth in what can only be described as a fight-*and*-flight response. She could, as promised by her trainers, obey twelve commands in Dutch and German, but somehow, the one command she'd apparently never mastered in any language was *Shut the hell up.*

I would describe myself as a mild-mannered guy, and I doubt that anyone would argue with that description. I've got my issues, but up until that day, anger had never been one of them. But the sight and sound of that fifty-pound, four-legged burglar alarm telling me to get off of *her* property really pissed me off. All of my pent-up grief, frustration, helplessness, stress—it all turned into anger, anger like I had never felt before, and I didn't need a doctor to tell me that it wasn't healthy. I went into my room and lay down until I stopped shaking, but every time the doorbell rang or a car came down the driveway or someone walked past on the street or our mailman came, that dog blew up. And every time that dog blew up, I wanted to kill it.

The most impressive display of barking came a few days after I'd come home, when my daughter Ava's guitar teacher came over for the weekly lesson. Kevin is as soft-spoken and easygoing a guy as you'll find anywhere. He's also African American. I learned that day that when our dog sees a black guy, she goes ballistic. Tell me what's wrong with this picture: Dark-skinned music teacher comes to the door, trained dog from North Carolina goes berserk, white owner tries—unsuccessfully—to control the dog by giving it commands . . . in German.

Nein! Sitz! Fuss!

The barking wasn't the only problem. The dog had separation issues. One night we tried leaving her alone in the house, and when we got back we found that she had forced her way into the girls' bedrooms, urinated on the carpeting in both rooms, and defecated there for good measure. She was having a lot of potty accidents in the house, especially at night. Since I'm the morning person, guess who stepped in it every time.

Out of fairness to the dog, I should point out that she was still new to our home, she had surely been abused before being abandoned, and she was only a year old and therefore still a puppy. She behaved perfectly around women and especially around children. When I walked her, she never barked at strangers or at other dogs or even at squirrels. If I told her to sit, she sat. If I told her to wait, she waited. And everyone who saw this dog told me she was adorable. "She's a movie-star dog!" was something I heard a lot. I assume it was meant as a compliment, but I'm married to someone who has worked with movie stars, so it doesn't sound like a compliment to me. Dog people say she looks like a gigantic West Highland white terrier. I think she looks like a dust mop.

Every morning during those dog days of summer, I got up before dawn, sat out in the backyard for a few minutes, and thought to myself, *Today is going to be a good day.* But then the chaos familiar to any parent with young kids would begin. The girls would start bickering, we would run out of milk, I'd open a cupboard and find it crawling with ants, a toilet would back up because someone had used too much paper, and no matter how hard I tried, it seemed I could never get the girls anywhere on time. They dragged their little feet and did everything at the last minute and could never find their shoes or their blankies or their hair bands or the brush that doesn't hurt when you use it. By ten every morning, I felt as if I couldn't take another minute of it, but there was no escape, and there were still ten hours to go until bedtime. And our bedtime ritual, which usually took about forty minutes, seemed to go on forever. It didn't help that by that time of night, I had already had several glasses of bourbon just to keep from losing my mind. And after putting the girls to bed, I still had to walk the dog and collect her stool in little plastic bags.

Then Erich called me with the results of Rachel's autopsy. It turned out that she didn't have an exotic virus from Central America after all. She'd entered the hospital with influenza— the flu—but on her second or third day there she got infected with staph, a highly antibiotic-resistant bacteria that has become endemic in hospitals. She may very well have lost her life because somebody forgot to wash their hands that day. If John Irving had done that to one of his characters in *The World According to Garp*, especially the mother of two little girls, I'd have thrown the book away a second time.

Twenty

TOWARD THE END OF JULY, Jessica surprised me with tickets for a concert at the Hollywood Bowl. The composer Philip Glass was scheduled to conduct a performance of his musical score for the movie
Koyaanisqatsi, and during the performance, the film was to be projected onto a giant screen behind the orchestra. We hired a sitter
for this one—Philip Glass is a minimalist, and so far, our children
seem to prefer maximalists in every category of human endeavor.
We brought a bottle of wine and some food and watched the sky
darken and the stars come out before the performance began. As
soon as the music started, I was hypnotized.

Koyaanisqatsi (a Navajo phrase meaning "things out of balance," and pronounced something like KOI-yah-ni-SCOT-sie) is a
wordless, plotless film. It's a series of glimpses of our magnificent
but troubled world—hundreds of them, seen through the lens of
a master cinematographer: canyons, cave paintings, deserts, for-
ests, cities, machines, insects, traffic patterns, smokestacks, esca-
lators, mushroom clouds—presented without explanation. The
music gives the film its emotional shape. As the music reaches
its climax, a rocket appears on screen. It takes off, all controlled
fury. It powers its way skyward; it is a perfect, flaming spear. But
then it is overwhelmed by its own power. Its fury catches up with

it and consumes it; it explodes. Whoever was filming the rocket launch chose to follow a single, jagged chunk of wreckage as it fell burning to Earth, and the music that accompanies this scene is a modernist requiem.

That night, as I watched that piece of flaming metal tumble through the sky, in slow motion and in total free fall, I started to cry. At Rachel's memorial service I had been unable to shed a tear, but at the Hollywood Bowl it finally happened. The movie ended, but I couldn't stop crying. I covered my face with my hands while the rest of the audience left the theater, and I kept my hands there as Jessica and I walked to the parking lot. I handed the keys over to her and cried all the way home as she drove. I cried as I undressed and cried until I fell asleep. The next morning, when I woke up, I felt better. But I didn't want to talk about what had happened or even think about it.

After seeing my reaction to that film, Jessica said to me: "I have an idea. It's been years since you've had time to yourself. Why don't you drive up to Idaho? You've always said you liked taking long drives by yourself. I'll take care of the girls. You can stay up there for a week, then I'll fly up with the kids to meet you there, and we'll all drive home together."

We have a dear friend up in Idaho with a guest house that we stay in when we visit him. I called Greg and asked if the guest house was available. He said he would be out of town, but yes, by all means, use the house.

But here's the thing: I felt sure that I couldn't relax on this trip knowing that Jessica would be working full time, watching both kids, and taking care of the dog without my help for ten more days. She'd just spent a month doing that while my sister was dying, and although Jessica never complains about anything, I knew that it hadn't been easy, and I didn't want her to have to do it again. So—believe it or not—I offered to take the dog with me.

It was my idea, not Jessica's or anybody else's, proving once and for all that I'm a moron. I thought that maybe, if I wasn't having to be a stay-at-home parent and grieving brother and panicked writer all at the same time, I might bond with the dog the way curmudgeons always do in heartwarming movies and bestselling books. I *wanted* that to happen. I didn't enjoy feeling the way I felt; I didn't want my kids to think that their daddy didn't love their new best friend. I was determined to turn things around. If I bring her to Idaho, I told myself, she'll lie at my feet and keep me company while I read and eat and nap and jot things down in my notebook. We'll take walks together every day. By the time we return to Los Angeles, we'll be inseparable.

When I take charge of things, they never unfold according to my wishes. If I had planned D-day, the Allies would have gotten lost in the Atlantic and stormed the beaches of New Jersey. On the drive up, Bowie and I stopped for the night at a dog-friendly hotel. I took her for a potty walk before we went inside, and I thought she'd emptied her tank, but the first thing she did when she got in the room was to squat and soak the carpet. When we arrived at my friend's house the next day, I kept her on a leash, even indoors, but it didn't matter. On our way to the kitchen, she froze as if she'd been shot, lowered her bum, and pissed right in front of me, half on the rug and half on my shoe, oblivious to the "*nein!*" and "*nay!*" commands and professionally approved corrective yanks on her training collar.

Greg's house is in the Wood River Valley, one of the most beautiful spots on Earth. Ernest Hemingway loved this area; his house is just up the road from where I was staying. Yes, he killed himself in it, but that's not Idaho's fault. Herds of elk wander around the neighborhood all the time. During my visits there, I have seen moose, red foxes, otters, and even a bear. The valley is far from any large cities, so there is almost no light pollution—the night sky is glorious. The Milky Way is stunning. On our first night there, I took Bowie out for a walk and tried to get her to look up. I wanted her to admire the portion of the Milky Way that runs through the constellation Sagittarius, the heart of our galaxy. Physicists say a giant black hole must be lurking there, gobbling up stars and space and even time and reducing all of it to a point of infinite density. Some days I wish we could all fall into it.

My dad used to take me out at nights with his telescope—the one he'd bitten off more than he could chew to buy—to stargaze. The hobby stuck; I've got my own telescope now, but when the sky is as clear and dark as it is in Idaho, you don't need a telescope to feel that you're spying on eternity.

The night sky makes me feel calm. All that empty space, the unimaginable distances between stars, makes what happens here on Earth seem relatively insignificant. Some people find that depressing, but I think it's cheering. It means our sorrows are small and they die with us, like raindrops dissolving into the ocean. Hemingway's suffering is ended now, but his better moments live on in his books.

My attempts to get Bowie to appreciate the Milky Way proved futile. If she couldn't eat it, or it hadn't come out of another animal's rear end, she wasn't interested. Back inside, she curled up on the floor next to the chair where I was sitting and fell asleep. She wanted me to like her, I could tell, and as long as she was asleep, I did like her. A little. We were going to make this work, one way or another.

The next morning, when I got up, I didn't have to make breakfast for the kids, and I didn't have to dress them or drive them to school or to playdates or doctor's appointments. I didn't have to entertain them or get them to brush their teeth or do their homework. I had only my own dishes to wash, no lunches to pack, no mail to answer, no bills to pay, no gutters to clean, no drains to clear, no ants to spray, no traps to set, no forced-air duct filters to change, no garbage bins to remember to drag out to the street before seven on Thursday, no toys to pick up, no groceries to buy, and no phone to answer. All I had to do was walk the dog, and then the day would be my own.

The moment I lifted her leash from the counter, she jumped to her feet. We do have this in common: We're morning people. I linked her up, and out the door we went, into the wild blue yonder, and it really is wild and it really is blue and it really feels like yonder up there. We walked about a mile south along the Big Wood River, and the only other people I saw were the fly fishermen in their waders, up to their hips in water that a day or two earlier must have been snow in the Sawtooth Mountains. There's a lovely path beside this river that used to be a railroad track. When the rail line got canceled, the residents of the valley decided to rip out the ties and the rails, smooth it out, pave it, and turn it into a walking trail. It's a twenty-mile-long gift. All it needs is a statue of Brad Pitt holding a fly-casting rod.

Bowie sniffed the ground. Was she going to do it? Was she going to poop outdoors and earn my undying gratitude? No— she'd found another dog's poop and seemed to be licking it. I groaned and gave her leash a tug. I looked up and saw a cyclist coming toward us, and I saw that he was moving fast. His head was lowered and his legs were pumping; he was not out there to admire the scenery—he was a serious athlete wearing a serious outfit. I had just enough time to reel in the dog's extendable leash and move off to one side. (The trail is only as wide as the train track once was, and I wanted to give this guy plenty of room.) I spooled in the leash cord and gave it a tug so that Bowie would move out of the center of the path, but that is the exact moment when she decided she had to defecate. And when this dog decides she is going to defecate, there is nothing you can do to stop her. Meanwhile, the cyclist was getting closer, and I could see that some of the push had gone out of his stroke. He saw how little room he had to get by the dog, and I'm sure he was wondering if this was the kind of dog that gets startled when a bicycle goes past her at twenty-five miles an hour at a distance of about six inches. I made a quick decision: I had to pull the dog out of the way. I dragged her, in that awful, scrunched-up shitting posture, her nails scratching across the pavement, as she left a trail of diarrhea across the trail. Nice.

The bicycle flew past us. Bowie looked at me guiltily. She was finished and was probably wondering if I was going to scold her. I didn't. I took out my little blue poop bag and scooped up as much of the mess as I could, but it was a futile task. The pristine walking trail was pristine no longer. We'd left our mark on the Wood River Valley.

But half a mile later, all was forgiven. We passed several other people walking their dogs, and I concluded that I was the only dog owner in that valley who used a leash. The off-leash dogs invariably rushed up to establish dominance, followed by much posturing and lurching and snapping, until their owners sauntered up without even bothering to lower their cell phones from their ears and said, "Oh, Max/Bailey/Cody/Duke/Cooper! Be nice!"

Bowie and I made it back to the house, where I gave her a treat, and then it was time to settle onto the couch with the view of the mountains and do what I'd been wanting to do for months: curl up under a blanket and get well. Bowie seemed to have the same idea, and that's exactly what she did, right next to the couch. And that's what we did together for four days, and it was good.

Twenty-one

ON THE FIFTH DAY, BOWIE stretched, sat up next to me, and rubbed her nose against my leg. She was blinding to look at—there was sunlight all over her fur. How did that sunlight get there? I know I'm having a good day when I don't even know if it's morning or afternoon. Bowie wanted to go out. She'd figured out the potty stuff by then. Good dog.

I put on her leash and took her out to the backyard, but then I decided, to hell with the leash, this dog needs a chance to run around for a while—she's not going to bother anybody.

A breeze rustled through the valley. The leaves on the aspen trees shuddered. Clouds drifted overhead and their round shadows raced across the hills. Bowie ran through the tall grass on the undeveloped lot next door, bounding over thistles and chasing things that I couldn't see. I'd never seen her run like this, and it was enjoyable to watch. She looked like a real animal now, not just a piece of living bric-a-brac. When she runs, she's fast and agile and even graceful. *What a pity it is,* I found myself thinking, *that she'll have to spend most of her life indoors.* She would be so happy as a working dog on a farm or a ranch or in the Arctic pulling a sled. Instead, like most AASFaDs, she'll have her daily walk and spend the rest of the day pacing and barking at doorbells. Poor thing.

She halted and started pawing at the ground. When she raised her head to look at me, I barely recognized her. Her head was no longer white, it was now the color of mud. Same with her paws. *Great,* I thought—with my luck, she'd probably dug into a water main and busted it. Or a sewer pipe. I called her over and wiped her off with a towel, and then I went to check on the damage. No pipes, just dirt.

I panfried a turkey and cheese sandwich in olive oil, washed some raspberries and grapes, poured myself a small glass of wine, and carried my movable feast outdoors. A bunch of dark clouds appeared over the hills, and within minutes they were overhead. The weather changes quickly in that valley. Halfway through my lunch, raindrops started falling, and I had to scurry indoors with my tray of goodies. Bowie and I were treated to the sight of an all-out Idaho downpour.

Rain used to depress me when I lived in Connecticut. It seemed to fall for months at a time there, but since moving to Los Angeles, I've come to feel differently about it. A storm, as far as I'm concerned, is a work of art. It has narrative structure. The one Bowie and I watched that day was a short story. It was over in around fifteen minutes, and that was just right. No Russian novels for me, thank you. The sunlight peeked through a break in the clouds, and I just had to laugh—there was a rainbow out there. Consider the fate of the rainbow, exploited for so long as a symbol of hope and innocence that you can't look at one anymore without feeling as if you're drowning in maple syrup! I tried to remind myself that rainbows don't have to signify anything. They are atmospheric phenomena that happen to be beautiful. I tried to look at this one with fresh eyes, but my mind wouldn't cooperate; it was like trying to look at a cross made out of wood without seeing a crucifix.

It was time for another glass of wine. I raised it in a toast to inactivity. Whenever I drink alone, I usually remember to toast someone or something. I can't remember where the habit started, but I'm in no hurry to break it. I made a resolution to do nothing at all for the rest of my vacation, just to see what it felt like. There was no rush, there was no deadline, there was no specific goal to be accomplished. That was the gift Jessica gave to me, and it would have been a shame to squander it.

Then I heard the sound of toenails scratching across wood. This was a new sound, unfamiliar to me—was Bowie trying to dig a hole in the floor? I turned around and saw that Bowie was trying to sit up. Her paws were sliding around on the floor as if she were on a sheet of ice rather than a wood floor. She looked drunk. Had she gotten into the liquor cabinet? She wobbled for a moment, and then she did something so strange that I didn't have any mental context for it at all, no category to put it into so that I could understand what was going on: She launched her torso upwards and balanced on her hind legs and rump like a circus performer, with her front paws extended in front of her. She teetered like that for a moment, went stiff as a board, and then dropped like a felled tree, landing flat on her back with her legs sticking up in the air. It looked so much like a parody of death that I wondered for a moment if it could be just that, an elaborate version of "play dead." Had her former owners, the ones who'd dumped her off by the side of a road somewhere, taught her this trick while they were waiting for their crystal meth to cook? Only when she flopped over to one side and drool started pouring out of her mouth did I realize that something was terribly wrong.

My mind stalled. I knew what I was supposed to be doing: rushing to the dog's side, cradling her in my arms, getting her to a veterinarian right away. I knew that this was what I had to do, but for a few agonizing moments, I could not do anything. I was paralyzed by disbelief; I found it difficult to accept that this was really happening. The whole scenario, beginning with my not wanting a dog to being strong-armed into getting one to having the dog arrive at the worst possible time and then my resenting it all out of proportion and now this preposterous medical emergency—after not one but several of my friends had remarked, in jest, that I'd better take good care of Bowie on my trip to Idaho because if anything bad happened to her it would look mighty suspicious—this was the plot of a Ben Stiller movie, not real life.

But then I remembered that this was my daughters' dog, not Ben Stiller's, and that cured my paralysis. I rushed Bowie to an animal clinic only two miles away, where a veterinarian looked Bowie over and said that it appeared she'd had either a seizure or a stroke or an aneurysm. Hard to say. "She might recover fully and never have another event, she might recover but with some impairment of function, the seizures could become intractable, or she might die in the next few minutes. I could tell you stories, but without all the information, it would just be guessing. For now, I'm going to run some tests and get her hydrated, and then we'll keep an eye on her and see what happens next." He took Bowie's leash off and handed it to me gently, and then his assistant picked Bowie up to carry her away.

Bowie looked at me—yes, *me,* the only person in the room who looked and smelled familiar to her—and tried to struggle free, but she was too weak. I returned to the house to wait for news.

Silence has a texture, and when I got back to Greg's house, I was reminded of how widely that texture can vary. An hour earlier, the silence in his house enveloped me like a down comforter. Now it was a vacuum that left me exposed. I paced through the house, trying to find a comfortable spot, but I carried my nakedness with me. I tried listening to music, but I was too agitated to concentrate. All I heard was noise.

I was agitated because I couldn't understand why I was feeling so upset. I kept seeing the look on Bowie's face when the vet's assistant carried her off, but instead of arousing my pity, it seemed to be unleashing something darker in me. Whatever it was, it wasn't directed at the dog; I wasn't angry at her for getting sick. I was afraid.

My sister-in-law once had a cat that was hit by a car. The cat survived but suffered nerve damage that rendered it unable to urinate without human assistance. For months, Jennifer dutifully brought the cat to her local vet's office twice a day to have its bladder manually squeezed. Eventually, Jennifer learned how to squeeze the cat herself, and she did this twice a day for years. Was this what was bothering me? Was I worried that I would be expected to squeeze Bowie's bladder for the next ten years or drive her to the hospital three times a week for dialysis or approve of an experimental surgical procedure that would require taking out a second mortgage on our home?

It was too damned confusing; I needed to stop thinking about it. I went to the shelf where Greg keeps his DVDs and browsed his collection. *Sense and Sensibility*? Too complicated. *Saving Private Ryan*? Too gory. *Planes, Trains and Automobiles*? Too frantic. I sorted through dozens of titles, but none of them appealed to me. I felt like a man on a cruise ship who was trying to distract himself from seasickness by checking out the buffet table.

But then I saw something there that surprised me, something completely unexpected: *Koyaanisqatsi*. The surprise came from the fact that since the film's release in 1979, I had never, ever seen a VHS or DVD copy of it in anyone's home. It's an arthouse film, for heaven's sake. Yet, only a couple of weeks after seeing it for the first time myself, here it was on Greg's shelf, and the moment I saw it, I realized that it was exactly the film I wanted to see. It occurred to me that if I watched it again, I might have that same cathartic experience—and I certainly could have used a cathartic experience just then.

I felt like an addict about to light an opium pipe; my hands shook as I slipped the disk into the player. I sat down on the couch and pressed the button on the remote, but I paused before the film started. I was shivering with cold; the chills were so intense that my whole body was trembling. I went upstairs, pulled the comforter off my bed, and brought it down to the couch. I curled up under a layer of goose down and pressed play again, and as soon as I heard the first note of the score, my eyes welled up. This time I wasn't in a crowd. I didn't have to feel embarrassed, I didn't have to hide my face in my hands, and I didn't have to drive home.

Twenty-two

BY THE TIME THE FILM ended, the lawn sprinklers had come on, and water droplets were hitting the window, sounding like rain, but the sky was cloudless.

I guess we all process information in our own way and at our own rate. When my nieces received the news that their mother had died, they could only hold that information in their minds for a few moments at a time. They were like stones skipping over the surface of a lake. They seemed to realize, instinctively, that if they thought about it for too long, they would sink.

Maybe we all do that. When I returned from Connecticut, I hardly thought about Rachel at all. It's not that I chose to avoid thinking about her, it's that my mind simply wouldn't go there. Some part of me sensed that the experience of losing her had been toxic. I buried the experience and then stood guard to make sure I couldn't dig it up. The problem is, you bury that stuff but the containers always seem to leak. Next thing you know, the lawn over your favorite park turns brown, and the lake catches fire.

Now I did want to think about my sister. I searched for her but she was hard to find. The most vivid memories I had of her were images from the hospital, when she was a corpse rather than a person, and from childhood, when she was painfully shy and withdrawn. That seemed unfair. I didn't want those to be my primary sources; I didn't want to remember my only sister that way. It's true, Rachel had struggled with anxiety and depression for most of her life, but that didn't stop her from achieving success in love and work. She had married, started a family, raised her girls, and run her own business. People adored her. I wanted to remember Rachel as a wife and mother and artist more than I wanted to remember her as a sister haunted by worries.

But like it or not, for me she had been reduced to a series of transparencies, a slide show in my mind. I couldn't change that, but at least I could try to choose my slides carefully. I adjusted my search terms. I looked for memories of her when she looked and felt free, and a few answered my summons. One was from that afternoon in Central Park, when she told me that since having a baby, she didn't feel so guilty about not making art anymore, and then tossed her head back and laughed. That became slide #1.

Another memory came from the party after her wedding. We had all moved from the reception site to the Tile Shop to whoop it up. As it was a tile store, the floors and walls had all been covered with pieces of ceramic; the room became a giant echo chamber, and the sounds of loud music and shouted conversation all blended together into a bright, noisy mess. When I find myself in noisy places, I tend to get overwhelmed and turn inward. I become oblivious to what's going on around me and shut down. I was doing it that night, when something caught my eye—someone was waving to get my attention. It was Rachel, in her wedding dress. She was gesturing for me to come over—hurry! I moved through the crowd and she pointed at something. It was our father, and he was dancing. He wasn't just dancing; he was going wild. He'd been jumping rope that year for exercise, and he was in great shape—the best shape of his life—and he was moving like none of us had ever seen him move before. A crowd had formed around him and was cheering him on. We all stared in amazement at this unprecedented spectacle. It wasn't just that he was being so physically active; it was that he looked so incredibly happy. Our father, who looked so incredibly *un*happy so much of the time. And of all three of us children, the one who most wanted our father to feel happy was Rachel, his daughter, because of all of us, she was the one who knew best what it was like to feel unhappy. Her wedding had brought about the miracle. She and I shared a glance, and the look on her face at that moment became slide #2.

A few more memories answered the summons, but then the source ran dry, and I ached because I knew that this was where it stopped. I knew this because the same had become true of my mother. She'd been dead for six years, and the slide show I had for her was pitiful. The images didn't even begin to represent what she'd meant to me when I needed her most. Of the tens of thousands of hours of her presence that I knew as a child, almost nothing was left. And someday, the same will be true of my relationship with my daughters. All that is going on right now between us—the shared discoveries, the unconditional love, the triumphs, the setbacks, the surprises, the delight, the awe—all of it will disappear. When I die, I will become a slide show just like my mother and sister, and when my daughters die, even that will be gone. There may be photographs and stories passed on to grandchildren, but these will have no emotional content, they will have no life.

I thought about the question I asked myself the day Rachel died: If I could press a button and make the human drama vanish without a trace, would I? My answer that afternoon was that there's no need to press that button. It's happening anyway— slowly rather than quickly, and painfully rather than painlessly, but it's happening. Everything is disappearing.

So if everything is going to vanish, what's the use of being afraid or angry?

I'd gone down this route before—*if you accept impermanence, then suffering needn't trouble you!*—and it hadn't made any goddamn difference. It's like saying that if you could just accept that

138

the compound fracture in your leg will heal eventually, the pain needn't trouble you. I'll take the morphine, thanks. But that afternoon, after watching *Koyaanisqatsi* for the second time, I wasn't feeling afraid or angry. I'd been squeezed dry. Then the phone rang. It was the vet.

He explained that Bowie seemed to be doing well. Normally, he would keep Bowie at the clinic overnight, but he had drive to Twin Falls to attend his daughter's wedding that night and wouldn't be able to help if Bowie had another seizure. It would be better, he said, if Bowie stayed with me so that if she had another event, I could rush her to the animal hospital in Hailey. If nothing happened during the night, I could bring her back to the clinic for a checkup first thing the next morning.

I wasn't happy about having to spend the night watching a sick dog, but I couldn't blame the vet. Here he was, working on the afternoon of his daughter's wedding day and planning to be back at work by eight the next morning. If he hadn't already been married, and if my sister-in-law who had squeezed her cat hadn't also been married, I would have tried to set them up.

I brought Bowie back to the house—she was wobbly but otherwise looked fine—warmed up some dinner, and took it to the study on the far side of the house. That room has my favorite view of the mountains. Bowie followed me. She was being very affectionate and clearly did not want to be left alone. When I sat down to eat, she seemed determined to keep some part of her body in contact with either my feet or my legs. Not even I could resist this. When I taught at juvenile hall, all it would take for one of the kids to win me over was to ask to sit next to me during class.

After dinner, I poked around Greg's shelves for another movie to watch. I picked an old, nine-part BBC television series about the development of Western civilization. It was written and narrated by an art historian, an adorably stiff British aristocrat who is identified only by his title, Lord Something-or-Other. I don't know how Lord Something-or-Other felt about life in general, but he sure knew how to appreciate art. He just loved the stuff, and for me, his enthusiasm was just what the doctor ordered. The first episode of the series is about ancient art—really ancient art: cave paintings, obelisks, pottery, pyramids. I never realized axe heads could be beautiful, but after hearing this guy gush about them, I became a convert. I got a little concerned that when Lord Something-or-Other got to the Impressionists, his head might explode.

Bowie stayed right in her spot on the floor as I powered my way through Lascaux and Byzantium, then I skipped ahead to the episode about cathedrals. I've always liked cathedrals, and something told me that Lord Something-or-Other was going to convince me to like them even more.

And I was right; he did. They are glorious places. They are the next best thing to staring up into the sky on a clear night. My spirits soared, and I sensed that something good was about to happen to me and Bowie. I felt certain of it. I could feel its approach, but I couldn't see it clearly yet. I didn't know what it was. Was it the healing power of art? I tried to get her to look at the screen, but with the same result as when I'd tried to get her to admire the Milky Way. Oh, well.

While Lord Something-or-Other exulted over the stained glass windows at Chartres, Bowie started panting. She was drooling again, and then she vomited. I watched to see if she was going to have another seizure, but she just panted and stared at me and looked, well, as sick as a dog. I tried keeping one eye on her and the other on Lord Something-or-Other, but the magic was broken. The possibility of having to drive Bowie to an animal hospital in the middle of the night made it difficult to concentrate, so I turned off the VCR and led Bowie into the bedroom and put her doggie bed at the foot of mine. She looked surprised, as if she couldn't believe her good luck—she was going to sleep in her master's bedroom! At last! Oh boy!

Oh boy. Her breathing was rapid and erratic, and the sound of it really got to me because it reminded me of the nights I had spent in Rachel's hospital room, listening to her labored breathing. And the sound of my mother gasping for breath when her lungs got filled with cancer. And of the night I had my first panic attack, when I felt as if I couldn't get enough air. Honestly, I didn't want to think about breathing anymore.

I didn't feel like reading, and I didn't feel like writing. All that was left was thinking, and that's risky business in the middle of the night when you can't get to sleep and you're vulnerable to episodes of acute anxiety. If my thoughts started racing, I would know that I was headed for trouble. I made a kind of chair out of all the pillows on the bed, and I propped myself up against the headboard. I'd learned from my ordeal in March that if I think a panic attack might be on the way, I mustn't lie down. When I lie down, my thoughts tend to drift around aimlessly; they don't coalesce, and when they don't string together properly, they become more likely to fly out of control. When I'm upright, I stand a better chance of warding off evil.

Warding off evil—that became my topic for contemplation.

Jessica had given me two books to bring with me on my trip to Idaho, both of them loaded with didactic significance. One was *Stickeen*, John Muir's story of a perilous hike across a glacier with a brave little dog as his companion. The other was *Travels with Charley*, John Steinbeck's account of his journey around America in a converted pickup truck with his dog Charley riding shotgun. Obviously, I was supposed to learn lessons from these books and apply them to my own life, but I found that I had too little in common with the authors to see them as role models. Muir was a fearless outdoorsman and Stickeen wasn't even his dog—at the end of the hike, Muir was able to give the dog back, cherish the memory, and live dog-free for the rest of his life. As for Steinbeck, his reason for making the trip was to get out of his comfort zone and rediscover the America that he'd gotten out of touch with since becoming a famous author. And he brought Charley along because he loved dogs. I, on the other hand, had come to Idaho

141

to *find* my comfort zone—a quiet, empty house—and put myself securely into it. I'd brought the dog out of a sense of guilt.

There was one story in *Travels with Charley* that did strike a chord with me, however. Steinbeck describes meeting a Filipino laborer who seemed unafraid of a place that Steinbeck felt must be haunted. The laborer explained that he was not afraid, because a witch doctor had given him a charm against evil spirits.

Steinbeck asked to see the charm, and here is what happened next:

> "It's words," he said. "It's a word charm."
>
> "Can you say them to me?"
>
> "Sure," he said, and he droned, "In nomine Patris et Fillii et Spiritus Sancti."
>
> "What does it mean?" I asked.
>
> He raised his shoulders. "I don't know," he said. "It's a charm against evil spirits so I am not afraid of them."

Wasn't that what I'd been looking for all my life? Some sort of charm, an antidote for anguish? I didn't have to know what it meant, I just needed for it to work. Was that too much to ask?

I could see the moon through the window. It looked brighter and clearer than I'm used to seeing it. My thoughts were starting to pick up speed. That, I knew, was not good.

I could picture myself at age thirteen, wearing a bathrobe and a bald-head wig so I could look more like a Buddhist monk, burning incense in the basement and trying to become one with the universe by thinking of nothing at all. Next I saw myself at age thirty-six, wearing a towel over my head and a tinfoil skirt around my waist. Then I saw myself at age forty-nine, having panic attacks while trying to meditate. You know what? I'm a one-ring circus.

I thought about how I seem to get stuck going round and round, thinking about insoluble puzzles in an ever-tightening spiral until I crash. What a colossal waste of time and opportunity and consciousness.

The panic attack was on its way. The first bloom of prickly heat appeared in the center of my chest, and my heart started skipping beats. *Oh shit!* I thought. *Here it comes.* And then something unexpected happened:

Bowie broke wind.

It wasn't a little toot. It sounded as if a three-hundred-pound man had just sat down on a fifty-pound, fur-covered whoopee cushion.

My first reaction was to feel annoyed. I thought, *Can't I get a break? I'm having a breakdown here! Do you think you could go fart somewhere else?* Then I remembered that it wasn't Bowie's fault; there was nothing she could do about it. Dogs don't fart on purpose. Then she did it again, and the smell of it hit me, and I just had to laugh, the whole situation was so absurd. This was the soundtrack to my personal crisis: a farting terrier. And that's when the idea struck me that changed the way I feel about dogs. The idea was *Bowie is an empty boat.*

I wasn't thinking that Bowie had become enlightened, like the ideal man described in the *Zhuangzi,* or that she was some sort of machine, like the battery-operated horse in Ava's bedroom. Dogs may or may not be spiritually advanced beings, but they certainly do have minds. Instead, I was thinking that Bowie's mind operates just as spontaneously as her bowels. Her moods, her intentions, and her actions are determined by circumstance, just as an empty boat's movements are determined by circumstance. And by circumstance, I mean the sum of all past and present conditions affecting her, including biological design, individual genetic inheritance, prior conditioning, and present environment.

Some of these factors are obvious, like the fact that she is a dog, which explains why her vocal cords produce the sound that annoys me so much. She was left at a shelter, which probably explains the separation anxiety. She was almost certainly mistreated by a man, which would explain why she freaks out whenever a man enters her territory. In any case, when Bowie barks, freaks out, or farts, she is not exercising what you and I would call *free will*. She is not morally responsible for what she does; she can only do what, in some sense, she must do under the circumstances. Blaming her for what she does makes no more sense than blaming an empty boat for where it drifts. And here's the feel-good part of it: If she is always doing what she must, then for all practical purposes, that is the same as saying she is always doing the best she can. When I thought of her in that context, my irritation with her dissolved.

Then she farted a third time, and by then my panic symptoms were gone. That's when I had the idea that changed the way I feel about humans:

The dog's not the only empty boat in this room. Count me in.

I didn't mean that I'd become enlightened, or that I was a mindless object that only *appeared* to be conscious. I felt, as strongly and clearly as I have ever felt anything, that none of what was happening that night—either in Bowie's gut or in my mind or anywhere in the world—was happening on purpose. Everything, including my own thoughts, seemed to be driven by a kind of impersonal momentum, the way gravity drives the planets through their orbits or the way instinct drives birds to migrate according to the seasons.

Ten years earlier, in a cabin in New Hampshire, I had come to the conclusion that the source of artistic inspiration must lie beyond the realm of conscious control. On the night of the farting dog, I took that idea one step further. I became convinced that the source of *all* inspiration and action must lie beyond the realm of conscious control. My lifelong desire to gain control over my own mind, and therefore my own destiny, had been as misguided as my attempts to make my book about a nun a bestseller.

I had a friend who used to take his parents' car, a 1966 Austin-Healey convertible, out every day for an hour-long drive through the back roads of Westport, Connecticut. Being a sixteen-year-old male driving an English sports car, he drove above the posted speed limit at all times. He soon noticed that by the end of these excursions, his buttocks had become quite sore. Curious about this, he paid closer attention to his body while he drove and made an interesting discovery: Whenever he steered the car around turns, he involuntarily tensed the muscles in his rear end. "I realized," he told me, "that I had this feeling that if I held tight onto the car seat with my ass when I went around curves, then the car tires would grip the road and I wouldn't crash."

That relationship between effort and control turned out to be an illusion. Once he realized the error in his thinking, he was able to relax his buttocks when he drove, and the pain in his ass vanished.

I may have suffered from a similar misconception. I had been clenching my mind for forty-nine years, thinking that this painful effort would keep me on the road and lead me to my chosen destination rather than a destiny chosen for me by others. Had it been necessary?

I led Bowie out to the living room, opened a couple of windows just in case she decided to provide further inspiration, and then watched the falling rocket sequence in *Koyaanisqatsi* once more. Bowie insisted on resting with her chin draped over my feet; if I tried to move them away, she whined. This time, as I watched the film, I felt I understood why I'd been so moved by that scene.

A conventional psychological interpretation would probably go something like this: The rocket's trajectory represents the course of a human life. Powering its way skyward, the rocket is like all of us as we go about the urgent business of trying to wrest ourselves free from the grip of circumstance and chart our own courses through life. The rocket is doing what any of us does as we strive to transform ourselves from mere animals into angels. Some of us do fly high, but not all of us are so lucky. Some of us break apart before we reach our goals (or a ripe old age), and we end up in a state of free fall, tumbling helplessly to Earth—dying young like my sister or becoming nervous wrecks like me. In the end, we all tumble to Earth anyway, whether we reach our goals or not.

Now I saw the rocket in a different light. I was in free fall as I watched it; the panic attacks had taught me that at the very core of myself I am not in control of anything. The attacks had brought me to my knees; they taught me what it means to feel helpless. Not only that: They taught me that I've been in free fall all along. I've always been in free fall. Everyone is in free fall, everything is in free fall. There is nothing but free fall.

When a rocket is climbing, it is in free fall. It looks to us like powered, controlled flight, but that's an illusion. The cascade of events leading to its launch, including the decision to build it, to fill it with fuel, and then to ignite the fuel, the series of chemical reactions lifting it off the ground, and the matrix of physical laws governing how it behaves as it moves through the sky—all of those forces act upon and through the rocket impersonally, irresistibly, as the result of a web of causality. We owe all of what we feel, all of what we think, all of what we do, and all of what happens around us to the spontaneous activity of that web.

My normal sense of being the author of my life-narrative gave way and was replaced by a sense that I was the audience for it. The author, I felt, had to be the cosmos as a whole, the vast matrix of who knows what and where and why, of which human consciousness is one part. From that point of view, I could no longer believe that we *determine* what happens to us, or choose who to be; we *find out* what happens to us. We do what we must as we fall through time, which means—this is the feel-good part again—that we are doing the best we can, always.

Twenty-three

TWO YEARS HAVE PASSED SINCE my epiphany in Idaho. Believing that we are always doing the best we can, whether we intend to or not, and whether we like it or not, has turned out to be my antidote for anguish. It's my comforting but unverifiable belief. I no longer think that I bear sole responsibility for who I am, what I do, or what I become. I share responsibility for those things with something infinitely larger than my conscious self—a higher power, which I call nature, although I don't have any objection if you prefer to call it God on my behalf. The experience of human freedom and responsibility loses some of its terrifying significance when it is placed in a larger context.

As for my imaginary button, the one that would bring the tragedy of human existence to a painless conclusion, in my present frame of mind I'd leave the button alone. I assume that the destiny of our species, tragic or not, is unfolding in a manner determined by natural law rather than supernatural forces or intentions. The same, I assume, must be true of my personal destiny. Believing that I'm a leaf in the wind comforts me, and when fear subsides, enthusiasm for life takes its place.

I call myself a futilitarian, which means that although I don't believe that anything I do really matters, I feel like doing it anyway. Among the things I feel like doing these days are saying no when my kids ask for more pets (Mom got them a pair of beta fish anyway, but if I'd offered no resistance at all it might have been another dog), answering the letters to Zeus and Hera that Esme tucks under her pillow at night (*D'Aulaire's Book of Greek Myths* made a big impression), and writing yet another draft of my novel set in thirteenth-century Asia. When Yin Lu and the Mongols stop haunting me, that's when I'll move on.

As for Bowie, she recovered completely from whatever it was that happened to her up there. She is fine as I'm writing this, and she is a happy dog by anyone's standards. I still get annoyed when she barks, but the annoyance passes quickly. We've tried two kinds of bark prevention collars on her, with mixed results. One delivers a mild shock, the other produces a citrus-scented mist that dogs find objectionable.

The shock collar was a bust. I tried it on myself, and believe me, you'll never hear me bark again. I've never seen Jessica laugh so hard as when she saw me hold that thing to my throat, go *"woof"* a few times without any result, grumble about having wasted our money, then yell *"RUFF!"* and get the surprise of my life. I don't recommend it. When we put it on Bowie, it just made her look more confused than ever.

The citrus version works better, but you're not supposed to keep it on the dog all the time, and the tiny battery is always going dead. A typical scenario: Bowie starts barking at the FedEx guy who needs a signature for a package. I go grab the collar, and she makes me chase her all over the yard until I've cornered her, and then I put it on her. I let go of her, and she starts barking again. Dead battery. I chase her down again, take off the stupid collar, replace the battery, and get it back on her, but by then someone else has signed for the package and the intruder is gone. Bowie wins again.

The girls love their dog and she loves them back. My brother-in-law, Marty, a single guy who adopts pit bull mixes from shelters, plops Bowie on his lap whenever he comes over—all fifty pounds of her—and lets her kiss him on the mouth. "Look how *happy* she is!" he announces.

"Get a room," I respond.

You're never going to see me with a dog on my lap, but I walk Bowie twice a day, toss her ball, scratch her belly, and give her treats. In return, she lets me know when music teachers invade our territory. For a pair of empty boats tethered together, we're doing pretty well.

My nieces are doing well too. They're getting ready to travel to Romania this summer with their dad to swim in the Black Sea, hike in the Carpathian Mountains, and visit their paternal grandparents. They sound cheerful whenever I talk to them. They are doing great in school and have outgrown Hannah Montana. If there is an afterlife, their mother must be proud.

Here in California, we've got a pair of birthdays coming up next week. Ava will be turning ten and Esme seven. Both girls want sleepover parties, so we'll have one this weekend and one the following. Jessica is all for it. I wonder: Couldn't we celebrate every other year?

Ava is our tomboy. Her current choices, in terms of who to be, are: heavy metal guitar player (she has already chosen a name for her band—Tone Death), artist (zombie themes figure prominently), skateboarder, fencer, and paleontologist. Her most prized possession is her skull collection. She is still serene, but sometimes I wish this kid was a little less serene about keeping track of her homework, her hoodies, and her trading cards. She loses everything.

Ava's serenity has earned her the nickname Buddha Baby. Her little sister is our Baby Bacchus. Esme is the conflicted one; she can go from joy to fury to sorrow to laughter in ten seconds flat. If there is humor to be found in any situation, or drama to be wrung from it, Esme will find it/wring it. One night, she got especially frustrated after being unable to provoke any of us into an argument at the dinner table. She'd tried pestering her sister, challenging her mommy, and browbeating her daddy, but no one was taking the bait that night. At last, she groaned like a wounded animal and blurted, "I wish somebody in this family was mean!"

I laughed and asked why she would want such a thing. She raised her clenched fists in the air and howled, *"So I can get what I need!"*

Esme makes no distinction between wishes and needs, so her list of unmet needs could fill volumes. Unlike her sister, she already seems to get it—that we can't always have what we want, or do what we want, or be who we choose to be. And she seems as puzzled by this as she seems outraged. "I want to be good," she once wailed after receiving her third time-out of the night, "but my body wants to be bad!"

Yet, at other times, she seems content to let things be as they are. She likes to take what she calls "life walks," where she and her mother stroll around the neighborhood and talk about, well, life. She invited me to join her for one of these walks recently, and after confessing that she felt bad about earning so many time-outs, she suddenly said, "Sometimes I get this feeling that maybe everything is supposed to happen."

When I asked her to explain this, she said, "Maybe the world is a big body, and I'm a cell! I'm just doing what the big body wants me to do!"

That's Daddy's girl! And I swear, I haven't said anything to the kids about being empty boats. I'm not allowed to; Jessica says I can't deny the existence of human freedom and responsibility in front of the girls until they've finished high school. And if I've learned one thing from being a dad, it's that you don't mess with Mom.

In the meantime, I figure I can teach by example. The example I hope I'm setting these days is that it doesn't hurt to believe that you're doing your best no matter what. When I screw up, I accept that I'm liable for the consequences, but in my heart I blame the cosmos, and that keeps my demons in line. Let's face it: I'm a free will denier and a moral relativist and my personal savior is a farting dog. No one's going to ask me to be their spiritual director or to run their school board. I have to believe I'm doing my best because I doubt anyone else will. Don't we all need someone who believes in us?

Copyright © 2012 by Mark Salzman
Cover design by Connie Gabbert
ISBN: 978-1-4532-5813-2 (paperback)
ISBN: 978-1-4532-2267-6 (hardcover)

Published in 2012 by Open Road Integrated Media
180 Varick Street
New York, NY 10014
www.openroadmedia.com

CPSIA information can be obtained at www.ICGtesting.com
Printed in the USA
LVOW091921160412

277784LV00003B/7/P

9 781453 258132